Praise for

"Angelica Stuart's *Chakra Anima*

tuitive, oracular, and divinatory tools. Its images are of animals and it speaks of their sacred power in the very energy centers that translate light to form: the chakras."

—Orion Foxwood, author of *The Faery Teachings*

"*Chakra Animals* is insightful, informative, and extremely readable. Angelica Stuart's love of the subject, and her readers, is obvious on every page."

—Richard Webster, author of *Is Your Pet Psychic?* and *Living in Your Soul's Light*

"We humans love to ally ourselves with other animals, and *Chakra Animals* allows us to internalize the energies of fifty different beings while using the seven primary chakras as a road map. Angelica Stuart provides an introduction to these valuable relationships, helping the reader understand some of the ways in which the animals can guide us through personal growth and spiritual development."

—Lupa, author of *New Paths to Animal Totems: Three Alternative Approaches to Creating Your Own Totemism*

CHAKRA ANIMALS

About the Author

Angelica Stuart has been a spiritual practitioner for nearly forty years. Her journey has incorporated many different paths, including traditional craft and shamanic studies, working with the archangels, being an observer of people, and, of course, working with the chakras as a way to connect with her first love—the natural world. She graduated from Maryland Institute College of Art with a BFA in drawing and continues to create things with her hands. She is a bit of a sci-fi geek, loves visiting wineries, and, when she isn't working or writing, loves to kayak on a calm lake or river.

CHAKRA ANIMALS

Discover Your Connection to Wisdom of the Natural World

ANGELICA STUART

Llewellyn Publications
Woodbury, Minnesota

First Edition
First Printing, 2019

Cover design by Kevin R. Brown
Interior animal illustrations by Eugene Smith
Interior chakra illustration by Mary Ann Zapalac

Library of Congress Cataloging-in-Publication Data
Names: Stuart, Angelica, author.
Title: Chakra animals : discover your connection to wisdom of the natural world / Angelica Stuart.
Description: First Edition. | Woodbury : Llewellyn Worldwide, Ltd., 2019.
Identifiers: LCCN 2018042876 (print) | LCCN 2018050472 (ebook) | ISBN 9780738759630 (ebook) | ISBN 9780738759593 (alk. paper)
Subjects: LCSH: Animals--Miscellanea. | Totems—Miscellanea. | Chakras--Miscellanea.
Classification: LCC BF1623.A55 (ebook) | LCC BF1623.A55 S78 2019 (print) | DDC 133/.259—dc23
LC record available at https://lccn.loc.gov/2018042876

Llewellyn Worldwide Ltd. does not participate in, endorse, or have any authority or responsibility concerning private business transactions between our authors and the public.

All mail addressed to the author is forwarded but the publisher cannot, unless specifically instructed by the author, give out an address or phone number.

Any internet references contained in this work are current at publication time, but the publisher cannot guarantee that a specific location will continue to be maintained. Please refer to the publisher's website for links to authors' websites and other sources.

Llewellyn Publications
A Division of Llewellyn Worldwide Ltd.
2143 Wooddale Drive
Woodbury, MN 55125-2989
www.llewellyn.com

Printed in the United States of America

For Turtle

Disclaimer

The material in this book is not intended as a substitute for trained medical or psychological advice. Readers are advised to consult their personal healthcare professionals regarding treatment. The publisher and the author assume no liability for any injuries caused to the reader that may result from the reader's use of the content contained herein and recommend common sense when contemplating the practices described in the work.

Author's Note

I made every attempt to include the most recent information and studies that I could find about the animals, but new studies and discoveries are constantly being made. If by the time you read this book a detail about an animal is outdated, I humbly apologize.

We are here to awaken from the illusion of our separateness.

—THICH NHAT HANH

Contents

INTRODUCTION

We share our world with many fantastic creatures, and each has a lesson if we are willing to listen. The yogis teach that we humans have four natural instincts: food, sleep, sex, and self-preservation. So it is in the animal world. The human is just another mammal, and if we can let go of our illusion of dominance, we can learn from the similarities we have with the cohabitants of the planet we share. For example, do you like to live in the woods, need to be near water, or live in a city, or can you live anywhere comfortably? Are you a loner or do you prefer to be part of a traditional family or family-of-choice community? Are you a meat eater or would you prefer to have seafood or a salad? Are you a night owl, only coming to life after the sun has set, or are you a morning songbird? Understanding commonalities on a fundamental level may help you deepen your connection with the natural world.

There are plenty of excellent available books and oracle systems that focus on the totem aspects of animals; I have quite a collection myself and use them regularly. What I've discovered, and perhaps you have too, is that the meaning of an animal often changes depending on location, culture, or belief system. For example, an owl in one culture means wisdom, but in another culture it represents death. How cultures view animals may change, but what doesn't change is the animal itself. Where does it live? How does it live? What does it eat? Just like animals, we humans have lifestyle preferences that change from person to person. My goal is to shed some light on potential similarities between you and a few animals by connecting your living habits via the chakra system.

The descriptions in this book are a combination of my personal experiences, observations, and research, but if you have personal experience with a particular animal, be it spiritual or earthly, honor the connection you have and use what you know. That animal is speaking to you directly. What I've written is merely a suggestion and may not match your experience. For the most part, I try to stay focused on the essence of the animal, but there are a few totem attributes filtered in as well.

I encourage you, if at all possible, not only to read up on any of the animals that call to you but also to spend time outside. Find a place you can sit still, watch, and listen. Are the birds talking to each other? Are the squirrels communicating? Even if you live in the city, there is wildlife. One summer night while I visited a friend in the mountains of Maryland, we witnessed thousands of fireflies communicating with waves of light through the trees. It was an amazing experience that we would have missed had we not been paying attention.

For this version of the Chakra Animals method, I focus on animals of North America because this is where I live. For clarification purposes, I use the term *animal* to represent anything nonhuman, such as birds, amphibians, insects, and other creatures. The way that I chose the animals was a combination of familiarity and research. Chakra Animals started out as a visual aid for a personal meditation practice. I shared that aid with a few friends, and they asked me to make sets for them. Knowing that I was going to be vending at an event in Massachusetts, I made a few prototype sets and offered to do readings for free to introduce the system. I created a form that listed about sixty different animals and asked people who visited my booth to check which animals they would like to see in a set and to add any animals that I hadn't named. After I tallied the responses, I came up with this current collection of animals.

The first version of the book was very small, with only about a sentence or two for each chakra. After doing readings at an event in Berkeley Springs, West Virginia, I realized that the book needed much more material, so I began its expansion. I don't presume to be a chakra expert, nor am I a biologist, but I have forty years of spiritual and magical practice that have led me to this system. I truly believe that I could not have written this book any earlier in my life, that all my life experiences have given me a foundation to present this information in a way that may be beneficial to others.

The way that I made the correlations between an animal and the chakras was through a combination of intuition and logic. As a starting point, I would research as much as I could about a particular animal, and for each I had a list of search criteria based on the core aspects of each chakra. I asked, where does it live? How does it live and with whom? What drives it? How does it communicate? Does it mate for life or not? These are all questions that relate to how we live our own lives, and the parallels fell into place. As I was writing, there were times I would often feel like I was channeling the spirit voice of the animal. Sometimes they had a lot to say, other times not so much. I am pretty sure that Archangel Ariel, patron saint of animals and nature, was occasionally whispering in my ear to get her message out into the world. Wherever the messages originated, I now share them with you.

What's Inside?

In the following sections, I'll discuss potential ways to use this book, a brief overview of the chakras, some suggestions and examples for practical use of the information, and how to do a reading if you choose to, and then I will introduce you to the fifty animals. In the back of the book is a list of possible connections between animals and themes (such as abundance, leadership, playfulness, etc.) that you might find useful. This list is by no means all-inclusive but may give you some insights. Before you dive into your practice, you may want to skip to that back section and skim through it to see if there is anything specific in the list that you are drawn to focus on. Also in the back of the book are images that can be cut out so you can make your own visual tool. You'll learn how to make use of that as we learn more about how to perform a reading in the chakras section of the book.

How to Use This Book

There are several ways you can approach this information. You can read the book from cover to cover and dog-ear and highlight places you want to return to. You can do a bit of bibliomancy and open the book at random to see what animal wants to speak to you. You can use the book in a similar way that you would use a totem guide, referring to a specific animal that has appeared to you or showed up in a dream. One practice I use is to pick an animal at random for each day of the week and connect that day to a chakra (Root: Monday, Sacral: Tuesday, etc.). The direct correlation may not be immediately clear to me, but it gives me food for thought as I move through the week.

My suggestion is to read all the animal descriptions, not just those for the animals you typically work with. Most of us who have worked with totem animals have a few we work with regularly, so we may not think about the possible connections we might have with others. I hope the information in this book surprises you with a few unexpected similarities with animals you had not previously considered. At the same time, I hope you discover a few surprises about your favorite animals as well.

My goal with Chakra Animals has been to try to help you understand that we are connected to the natural world in very down-to-earth ways. I hope you find this perspective fun and illuminating, and I also hope you have as much fun working with it as I've had developing it. It has indeed been a labor of love.

THE CHAKRAS

The word *chakra* (pronounced cha-krah) comes from ancient Sanskrit Vedic texts and loosely translates to mean anything that has a circular motion. For example, *cakravata* is a "whirlwind," and *kalacakra* means the "wheel of time" or "wheel of fortune."

The Kundalini chakras are what most people think of when they think of chakras. These chakras are energy centers that travel along the spinal region of the body from the base of the spine to the top of the head. Some traditions say there are five, some seven, others eight, and some over a hundred. For the purposes of this book, I use the seven chakras that are familiar to most people. While they are listed below in the descriptions, I don't reference the colors in the animal section because my focus is the core attribute of that chakra.

One of my favorite ways to understand chakras is by comparing them to individual pools of water along a stream. For us to remain mentally, physically, emotionally, and energetically healthy, those pools of water must be clean and free of debris so our energy can flow between them. Just like a river, if there is a blockage, the water dams up and collects all sorts of garbage. We can even become physically ill.

How we see the world, how the world sees us, everything we feel, everything we taste or touch, our gut instincts, our sense of security, our ability to manifest our dreams, our ability to communicate, and our ability to love and be loved can all be tied to our energetic health. I hope seeing your energy centers from a different perspective will help you to find balance and happiness.

The following are descriptions of each chakra. They are by no means all-inclusive, but they may be a useful reference while working with the animals.

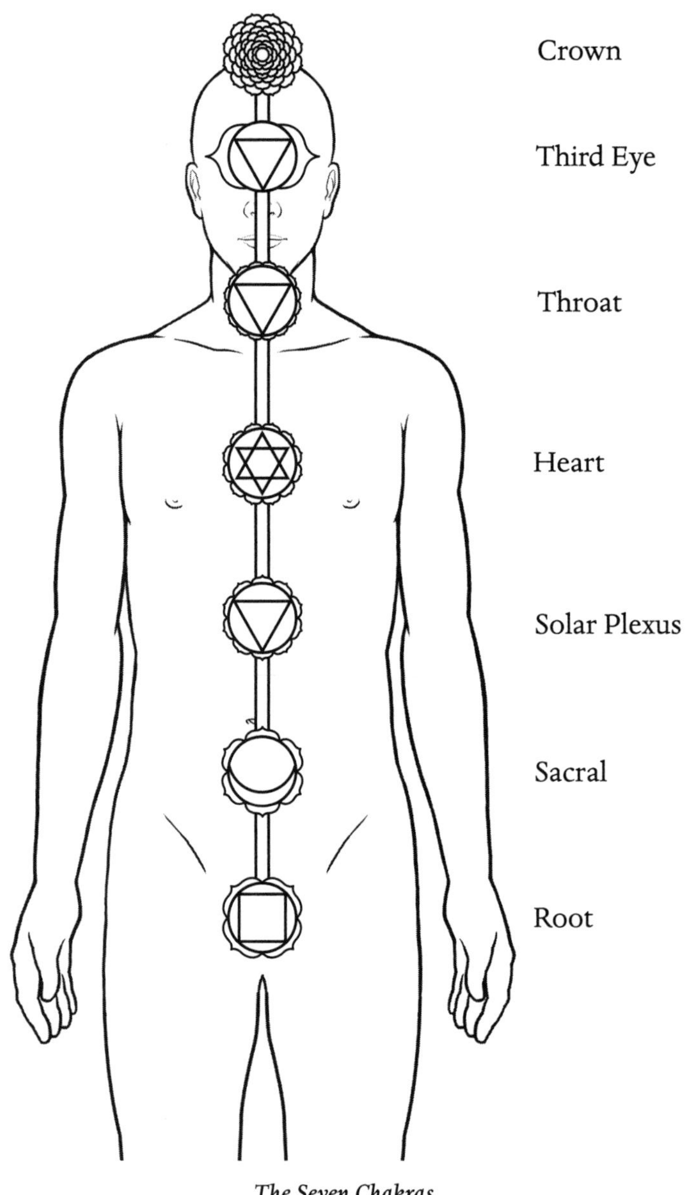

The Seven Chakras

Root Chakra

Color: Red • *Element:* Earth • *Sense:* Smell

The location of the root chakra is roughly an inch above the tailbone. This chakra connects you to the earth and helps you feel grounded and safe. It is your firm foundation and speaks to your primitive instincts and your senses of security, safety, and survival. It also speaks to basic life needs like food and home. It helps you tap into your body's needs.

Health in this chakra means that you feel grounded, safe, and secure in your life and living situation and that you are able to feel trust. If this chakra is out of balance, you may be fearful, detached, or even angry. This chakra stores some of your earliest emotional memories. If you grew up in a family feeling safe, sheltered, and rarely hungry, you probably have a healthy root chakra. However, if you grew up knowing only fear and want, or if you have ever been in an abusive relationship, this chakra may be damaged or hypersensitive.

The sense tied to this chakra is smell. Our sense of smell is one of our fundamental survival instincts. For example, if we smell fire, we run for safety. Most of us can smell if food has gone bad, so we know not to eat it because we might get sick. But if a person loses their sense of smell, they may not be able to tell if food has spoiled. Some animals will starve if they lose their sense of smell. There are some people whose sense of smell is so acute they can detect illness on another person. Some animals are trained as therapy companions to identify things like insulin imbalances and alert their humans that medication is needed. We often say that something just "smells wrong," so we avoid it. Smell helps us survive.

Other aspects key to your survival include knowing where you like to live and what makes you feel safe. Do you like living in a traditional family structure or with housemates, or are you more comfortable as a loner? How do you like your home to be? Do you prefer a tidy, well-organized space, or are you more comfortable with a bit of homey clutter? What do you like to eat? It is essential to understand and feed your basic needs so that you can not only survive but also thrive, and you do that through the root chakra. If you currently don't feel safe or aren't happy with your living situation, this chakra can help ground you so that you can see the life changes you need to make.

Sacral Chakra

Color: Orange • *Element:* Water • *Sense:* Taste

The location of the sacral chakra is in the sacrum, just below the belly button. The sacrum is the upside-down-triangle-shaped bone between your lower back and your rear end. This chakra is your pleasure center and speaks to your emotional body, sexuality, passions, desires, creativity, confidence, and self-worth. It is your ability to be open and friendly.

Health in this chakra means you are in touch with what makes you happy. It means your creative juices are flowing, and you have healthy emotional and sexual boundaries. You are easily able to express your desires. If this chakra is out of balance or blocked, it can manifest in many ways, including obsession, guilt, an explosive temper, or lack of creative energy. It can also manifest as either sexual addiction or repression. It is the difference between being able to relax and being unable to, between being confident and being arrogant, between living your passion and living in a shell.

The sense connected with this chakra is taste. For many, this sense is a source of pleasure; however, what pleases one person may not please another. Being in touch with what gives you pleasure helps you feel truly alive. While the root chakra speaks to your sense of physical security, this chakra speaks to your emotional security.

Solar Plexus Chakra

Color: Yellow • *Element:* Fire • *Sense:* Sight

The location of the solar plexus chakra is in between the base of your sternum and your belly button. This chakra is your power, energy, vitality, self-esteem, and ego. It is your ability to choose an intention and then take action to turn it into a plan. It is your gut instinct and your inner fire. This chakra is your relationship to the world around you and your comfort level about your place in it.

Health in this chakra means that you know who you are. You project confidence without being egotistical. You can work with others without needing to control a situation. If this chakra is out of balance, you may seem painfully shy or, on the opposite end of the spectrum, narcissistic. It may mean that you feel like nothing can get done unless you do it.

The sense connected to this chakra is sight, and it helps you realistically see the world. It means you can see the forest *and* the trees. This chakra enables you to stay in touch with the world around you so that you don't become someone who spends too much time navel-gazing. This chakra helps you see beyond just the plan to the completion of a project.

If you want to walk through the world with your head held high and confidently express yourself, tap into this chakra for strength.

Heart Chakra

Color: Green • *Element:* Air • *Sense:* Touch

The heart chakra is located behind the breastbone and is all about balance. It is the link between your lower three chakras (the place of your physical self) and the upper three chakras (the place of higher thought, dreams, and intuition). The heart chakra represents unconditional love, relationships, compassion, well-being, and spirituality. It connects the body and mind with Spirit.

Health in this chakra means that you can be emotionally open, loving, and compassionate. It says that you are in touch with your physical and spiritual needs in equal measure. You feel happy, peaceful, and friendly, and people see you as having an easygoing and forgiving personality. If this chakra is out of balance, you may feel overwhelmed by sorrow and have a desire to hide from the world. You may be intolerant of most everything, angry, irritable, and nasty. You may suffer from nightmares and have trouble feeling grounded. You may even feel short of breath or suffer from high blood pressure.

It will be no surprise that the sense connected to this chakra is touch. Touch is how you express your love and affection, be it by hugging someone, rocking a child, stroking your companion animals, or holding hands with the one you love. The act of touch is incredibly healing, and it is not unique to humans.

Many believe this chakra is the one that is most easily and frequently damaged but also the one that seems to *want* to heal. If your heart needs to heal, get outside among green things and breathe deeply. Snuggle with the one you love, human or animal. It may take time, but, believe me, I know as a widow and cancer survivor that your heart can heal.

Throat Chakra

Color: Blue • *Element:* Ether • *Sense:* Hearing

The throat chakra is located in the neck and aids you in your ability to communicate. It is important to remember that authentic communication is a two-way street. Being able to listen, *really* listen, is often more important than the words that come out of your mouth. This chakra is the place of self-expression, self-discipline, and your ability to take a creative idea and bring it out into the world. It is the power of sound and breath. This chakra is also where you consume food, so it is important to only let things through that will nourish you.

Health in this chakra means that you can speak your mind without cruelty and that you take your time to hear what another person is saying without focusing on your response. It means that you can bring your ideas and projects to fruition. It means that you can express yourself in a variety of ways, including but not limited to art, music, dance, writing, speaking, and thought. If this chakra is out of balance or damaged, it could mean that you suffer from stage fright, have a tendency to talk very loud or too much, and even interrupt while someone is talking. It is also possible that you have a collection of unfinished projects lying around.

The sense connected with this chakra is hearing. As stated above, listening is essential to authentic communication. It is important to listen to another's truth, but it is equally important to hear and understand your truth as well. Call on this chakra when you need to express yourself in any way, want to finish a project, or want to learn to shut up and listen.

Third Eye Chakra

Color: Indigo • *Element:* Light • *Sense:* Intuition

The location of the third eye chakra is in the center of the forehead. From here, you see the physical world with clarity, and it is also the seat of your intuition, insight, and focus. It is the place of wisdom and knowledge. It is your connection to your own higher self and the place of your psychic ability, where you see visions. While the solar plexus is the place of your gut instinct, the third eye is your intuition.

Health in this chakra means your intuition is reliable and accurate. It says you can visualize easily, have powerful insight, have excellent recall, and can remember your dreams. If this chakra is out of balance, you might suffer from nightmares, have trouble concentrating, and lean toward unhealthy or obsessive thoughts.

The sense connected to this chakra is intuition. Your intuition can be a powerful tool if you can silence the chaos of your inner chatterbox. Call on this chakra when you are looking for new ideas, are trying to gain a clear perspective of where you are in your life, want to improve your memory, or want to improve your psychic ability.

Crown Chakra

Color: Violet • ***Element:*** Thought • ***Sense:*** Consciousness

The location of the crown chakra is at the top of the head and is your connection to Source, Spirit, God—however you perceive the Divine. It is here that you receive cosmic awareness, enlightenment, and pure light. It allows for the inward flow of cosmic wisdom and is the gateway to other dimensions. The place from where you can travel on the astral plane.

Heath in this chakra means you are in touch with your divine source and you can walk through life with a sense of grace. You tend to have a calm presence and can see beyond the big picture. You can quickly assimilate and analyze complex information, and you have a broad and far-reaching understanding of life itself. If this chakra is out of balance, you might be cynical about anything you can't touch or see, or you might experience the opposite of that: an addiction to meditation or some other spiritual practice, focusing too much on spirit realms and forgetting to stay grounded or pay your bills.

The sense connected to this chakra is consciousness. It is how you see beyond your human perception and existence to something greater than yourself. Tap into this chakra to connect with all that is.

PRACTICAL USES

Finding animals that you resonate with on a practical level can be fun and can potentially enhance your spiritual practice by expanding your pool of animal collaborators. Another usage could come when you are struggling or working on areas of your life or trying to make changes; find an animal that has attributes you admire and try to incorporate those attributes.

For example, if you have trouble communicating and words tend to get stuck in your throat, it could be because of fear, your thoughts getting ahead of you, or you feel pressured by an outside influence. If fear is what is causing you to climb in your shell like a turtle, try working with an animal that is the embodiment of courage, such as the mountain lion. If words tend to get stuck in your throat, consider working with the heron. Herons are very confident, patient birds. They will wait patiently at the water's edge, undistracted, until the timing is perfect, and only then do they straighten out their long S-curved necks to nab their prey. A takeaway lesson could be that you need to slow down, take a breath, refuse to be rushed, and speak only when you are ready. Doing so may help you build your confidence, and at the very least it will give you time to get your thoughts clear so that when you do speak, it is with forethought and dignity.

Another example is healing a broken heart. When we have been hurt, it is natural to want to wrap ourselves in protection for a while. The armadillo has a protective outer shell that can guard you when you need it. When you feel like you are ready to cast off that shell, transition to something like the butterfly so you can break through your chrysalis and fly.

There are endless parallels that I could make, but my hope is that you find many on your own. If you are having trouble, reference the

"Connections" section at the back of the book to see if any specific animals and their correlations resonate with you.

How to Do a Reading

While they aren't essential for working with this information, the animal illustrations shown throughout the book are also presented in the back of the book in the "Animal Images" section. If you would like to have some visual representation, as you would with tarot or other oracle systems, you can use the illustrations as they are, cut them out, or glue them to cardstock or wooden disks so they are durable. If you would like to order a deck of cards, a version is available with my artwork through either my Facebook page or my Etsy site. You can find this information in "How to Order a Deck" at the back of the book.

Here is a suggested method for a reading:

Place all the slips of paper in a bag or in a box and randomly pick one at a time, or spread all the slips of paper out facedown and pick that way. Center yourself in whatever method works best for you. With your eyes either open or closed, slowly move your hand over the pieces of paper until one feels *right* and place it face down on the chakra space that also feels *right*. Repeat this for each chakra, keeping all the images face down and in a row of seven to represent the seven chakras, until you have filled all the chakra spaces.

Starting with the root chakra (the first), turn over the image to see what animal has come through. Move on to the second, third, fourth, and so on. There is no "tradition" connected with the Chakra Animal method, so please explore it in ways that work for you. Most of all—have fun!

THE ANIMALS

ANT

Considered pests by nearly everyone, ants can be found all over the world except in the Antarctic (despite the name). The ant has a unique physiology that allows it to lift objects many times its body weight. Another unique detail is that an ant's central nervous system consists of a nerve cord that flows from its head to its rear, similar to a human spinal cord; it is as if they have a natural chakra pillar.

Key Attributes

Strong community ties, doesn't give up when the work is hard, willing to carry more than one's share, achieving goals, and planning for the future.

Chakra Interpretations

Root

An ant's survival depends on living in a colony with a clear social structure. You can live pretty much anywhere as long as you are part of a community of like-minded souls. If you find yourself alone for too long, you may start to question your self-worth and might even fall into depression. Get out and discover people with whom you can work or play. If where you are earning your living doesn't give you the satisfaction of shared success, you may need to look for a new job or try volunteering with a group for a shared benefit. The important thing is to find ways to be with other people who are working for a common goal.

Sacral

Humans are attracted to other people, be it sexually or platonically, via pheromones. These airborne molecules cause a reaction within members of the same species and are the chemicals responsible for the connection within an ant colony. When you first meet someone, either you immediately like that person or you don't. If you have a life partner, when you met this person, the attraction was probably instantaneous. If you aren't in a relationship but would like to be, it may be time to open your pheromone radar! If you have been feeling like you can't follow your creative passions because work is all you do, take a break and spend time with your musical instrument, your paintbrush, or your pen. Doing so may help you feel more complete.

Solar Plexus

When you watch a colony of ants working, it is as if you are observing a single entity. Ant in this chakra shows that you work well with others and you know your place within that social structure without letting ego get in the way, even if you are the leader. You are also willing to carry way more than your weight to ensure the work gets done. This singular focus can mean that you lose sight of the world around you, and if this is the case, try asking for help or delegating work to someone else. Remember, you don't need to do everything yourself. Look up from your work now and then so you see the beauty of the forest and not just the leaf you're struggling to carry.

Heart

Ants communicate information by touching each other's antennae or head. Most likely, you are the kind of person who likes to make physical contact when you talk to someone. Touch comes as naturally to you as breathing does for others. It may even be that you feel uncomfortable around standoffish people, wondering if you did something to offend them. Most likely, the other person isn't as comfortable with touch as you are. If you are concerned that you have offended someone or made them uncomfortable, ask them. Try gently explaining that this is how you connect to people. Clarity can sooth many perceived offenses.

Throat

Ants are team players, and clear communication is essential for the whole to function. In addition to using touch to communicate as mentioned above, an ant "hears" by feeling vibrations in the ground using sensors on its feet and knees, enabling it to interpret signals from its environment. Most likely, you tend to be one who listens, taking the time to pick up the vibe or energy of a gathering or meeting before you speak. This is a very wise and useful skill to have. You understand that miscommunication is unproductive. If you find yourself in a situation where things aren't getting done in an effective way, it may be time to share your wisdom with those who are doing more talking than listening.

Third Eye

Like most insects, the ant has compound eyes, which means it has hundreds of lenses that combine to form a single image in the ant's brain, similar to the way many pixels form an image. You are capable of understanding multiple sides of a situation and often perceive with a depth that others don't. You may also be extremely sensitive to the smallest energetic or empathetic vibration, which can sometimes make you feel overwhelmed, especially if there is no apparent reason for those feelings. If you live in a city or work in a high-stress job, this may be a frequent occurrence, and you may need to find something that can act as a mental shield for you, such as your name badge if work stress is the culprit. If you think you are picking up energy from your neighbors, try a mental image of a bubble within your living space that only you and whomever you choose can pass through.

Crown

As mentioned in the opening paragraph, an ant's very physiology has a direct parallel to chakra work due to the nerve cord that flows from its head to its rear. Interestingly, the ant breathes not with lungs but with tiny holes called *spiracles* that are located around the sides of its body. When you meditate, try breathing with your whole body. Feel the energy of the universe tingle your skin and vibrate your core. Feel life energy rise, starting with your feet, up your spine, and out through the top of your head. Ant energy may help you touch beyond the limitations of your physical body.

ARMADILLO

The Aztecs called them *turtle rabbits*, but the name *armadillo* is Spanish for "little-armored one." Armadillos live in warmer climates and build their burrows in areas that give lots of natural protection. Despite their lumbering gait, armadillos can run very fast, are excellent swimmers, and can hold their breath underwater for long periods of time. To escape a predator, they are able to walk across the bottom of streams instead of staying visible on the surface. Contrary to popular belief, only the three-banded armadillo can curl up into a ball. The nine-banded armadillo is the only species found in the United States and is the official state small mammal of Texas. An interesting fact is that nine-banded armadillos give birth to identical quadruplets, all fertilized from one egg.

Key Attributes

Understanding boundaries, both yours and others'; wearing defensive shields; playful innocence; and achieving goals despite obstacles.

Chakra Interpretations

Root

Armadillos are solitary creatures. Within their homes, they dig numerous holes and interlink them with an extensive system of semipermanent tunnels. Most likely, you are happiest living alone in a warm climate and feel safest when you have a network of places that you can escape to if need be. Another interpretation for the armadillo in the root chakra has to do with the fact that armadillos are nocturnal and only forage for food at night. It could be that you are the kind of person who wakes up in the middle of the night and raids the refrigerator. It could also be that you prefer working the overnight shift, or if you are in a business that allows flex time, you use it to your advantage by working late at night. If you are a student, you might do most of your studying during this time. Use your nocturnal preference to full advantage, because it is when you are at your best.

Sacral

If an armadillo can't climb over an obstacle, it will dig under it. When it comes to what drives you, you are willing to dig deep to find the information you need or even sidestep your way around obstacles without injuring or climbing over another person to reach your goals. The easygoing, playful, but solitary nature of the armadillo says you can easily entertain yourself. You don't feel the need to fit in or take part in activities that don't interest you just to be with other people. Armadillo energy protects your boundaries but asks if those boundaries are keeping you from being able to play.

Solar Plexus

Armadillos are the only mammals with a body covered in a hard shell. When frightened or startled, the nine-banded armadillo will jump straight up into the air several feet. Have you closed off to what is going on around you? Do you tend to be so focused on the task at hand that if you hear a loud noise or someone startles you, you jump out of your skin? Perhaps your shell is so thick you are not able to sense what is going on around you. There is a chance that some might misunderstand your solitary nature as being aloof. If this is not how you want people to see you, it may be time to let them see your softer, more playful side.

Heart

Baby nine-banded armadillos are born with soft shells; it takes several weeks for the armor to harden. If you feel like life events have caused you to develop a shell over time, the armadillo is a good animal to work with to remind you that you still have a softer side. Working with the armadillo can shield you until you are ready to trust enough to open your heart again. At the same time, if you are in a situation where the weight on your heart is taking its toll, use the armadillo's energy to wrap you in its shell until you can feel safe again.

Throat

Armadillos are not very vocal. Most only make grunting sounds as they forage for food. One species, the screaming hairy armadillo, is known for the loud shriek it makes when startled or annoyed. If you are shy or suffer from stage fright, wrap yourself in armadillo's shell while you try to find your voice. At the same time, avoid being the reverse of this—don't scream at people because you are hiding the fact that you are petrified. It is better in the long run if you face your fear head-on. You might discover that what scared you won't hurt you and can be a source of entertainment.

Third Eye

Armadillos stay in the shadows. They have very poor eyesight, so they rely on their sense of smell to find prey. They also have tiny hairs on their sides and bellies that help them feel their way around in the dark. You are the kind of person who depends on not only what you *see* but also what you *feel*. Armadillo energy encourages you to use your intuition and exceptional senses to explore your way around situations. You pick up things that other people are blind to and can sniff out secrets and mysteries that other people are missing.

Crown

Armadillos sleep for up to sixteen hours every day and only come out in the early morning or at night to forage for food. As mentioned earlier, nighttime is when you are most alive. If you work nights and need to sleep during the day when most of the world is active, it may be difficult for you to connect with Spirit or your dreams. If so, try wearing a sleep mask and installing blackout curtains in your room. Another possibility is that you have lost your faith or trust in your concept of a higher power and have developed a shell to block it. This can happen for any number of reasons: family issues, a bad experience working with a spiritual group, or simply lack of time. If you decide that reopening that connection is important to you, it is as easy as dropping the shell. While you *can* do it alone, take the risk and seek out others who share your spiritual ideals.

BADGER

Badgers are part of the Mustelidae family. There are several species of badger, and each has qualities that are unique to that species. While the European badger digs deep warrens that generations might occupy without interruption for decades or even centuries, the American badger is nomadic and moves across the landscape, digging a new burrow every day or two, and both species tend to keep their warrens very clean. A third species, the honey badger, is vicious and will just take over someone else's home. The honey badger is so vicious it is listed in the *Guinness World Records* (as of this writing) as the world's most fearless creature. The honey badger is in fact a separate genus from the American and European badgers and is more closely related to wolverines and weasels. A badger's behavior also differs by family; some are solitary, while others are known to form clans that last for many generations. Regardless of type, badgers have few, if any, natural enemies. Their low-slung bodies and powerful jaws and claws make it nearly impossible to topple them, and anything that tries quickly regrets it!

Key Attributes

Aggressive self-expression, leadership, courage, bravery, authority, perseverance, and achieving goals through determination.

Chakra Interpretations

Root

Most badgers are omnivores, so most likely your diet is diverse. However, the honey badger is a carnivore, so if that is the badger you connect with, then your preference is for meat, period. Like the badger, you are very tidy and organized but can be viciously territorial. Juvenile badgers grow up quickly and are ready to go off on their own by about five to six months. It is entirely possible that you became independent at a very young age, much younger than your peers. Badgers are powerful diggers, and in some shamanic traditions they are the keepers of medicine roots. You probably have a green thumb and would do well in the healing arts or as an herbalist. At the very least, people are probably envious of your garden.

Sacral

Badgers are quick-tempered and fiercely independent. Everything you do, you do with an all-consuming passion; subtlety is not even in your vocabulary. Most people don't know how to deal with your intensity, but this is your strength, so don't let anyone stop you. Most likely, you have an unrelenting drive and will stop at nothing to achieve your goals. If you are in the medical field or involved in any form of research, your intense focus means that you will dig, often using unconventional means, to find a cure for illness, the answer to a mystery, or the truth in any situation.

Solar Plexus

In addition to badgers' thick skin, they have a very commanding presence. Very little penetrates your tough exterior. You are very confident, but be careful that it is not to the point of arrogance. Anyone who knows you knows that you are not someone to cross, often to the point where they walk on eggshells so they don't invoke your wrath. However, a positive side to this confidence means that when confronted with a challenging situation that would confound most people and cause them to give up, you dig in your claws and get the job done.

Heart

The European badger's clan structure can last many generations, even centuries. It is possible that your heart feels a powerful pull to your ancestral past. If you don't already know your family tree, researching it could bring a great deal of satisfaction by helping your heart feel connected to your roots. Another key aspect of the badger in this chakra is a similarity to the skunk. When startled or threatened, badgers release an intense musky odor. As mentioned above, if people do tend to walk on eggshells around you, it might be that they are afraid of your temper or that you are stinking up your environment with a bad attitude. If you want to draw people closer to you, take a breath and try to not be so reactionary.

Throat

A badger can accomplish anything it sets out to do. Manifesting your goals and desires is never a problem for you. As mentioned above, if you connect with badger, you will dig deep to find a solution to a problem and will fight tooth and nail for something important to you. If you are a lawyer or someone who fights for a cause, badger in this chakra can be a powerful ally. A warning: a downside of the badger is using your voice for cruelty or control. If you are in a leadership or supervisory position, be mindful of how you treat those answerable to you. You may find that if you are mindful, people will be more willing to cooperate and give you what you want instead of resenting you because of your aggression.

Third Eye

Adult badgers have a third pair of eyelids that protect their eyes while they dig in the dirt. If you have badger in this chakra, you might be looking at the world through thick filters. You might have become so focused on your own perspective that you find it hard to see anyone else's. It could also be that something in your life is too hard to face and you don't want to look at it. If this is the case, use the badger's strength and courage to help you. From a strictly practical perspective, perhaps glaucoma runs in your family, and if so, you should have your eyes checked regularly.

Crown

While they aren't true hibernators, badgers are very inactive during winter months. They spend much of that time in the equivalent of a deep sleep or trance. Badger in this chakra is telling you that the winter months could be a powerful time for you to connect with the underworld and the mystery of creation.

BAT

Scientists have found evidence that bats have existed for at least fifty million years and possibly longer with very little change. There are well over nine hundred different species of bats worldwide, ranging in size from the tiny bumblebee bat to the huge Bismarck flying fox. Bats can be found everywhere except for the coldest climates and represent one-fifth to possibly even one-quarter of the world's mammal species. Bats are the only mammals capable of actual flight. Most bats emit sounds that return echoes, which they use to instantly determine the size of an object and how far away they are from it. Some bats roost alone or with a few others, but due to their social nature, most prefer to sleep in bigger groups. The largest bat colony in the world is in Bracken Cave, located near San Antonio, Texas. During the summer, this cave is home to as many as fifteen million Mexican free-tailed bats. The term *blind as a bat* is not accurate, nor is it fair: bats have excellent vision for seeing in the daylight. They just rarely come out before the sun sets.

Key Attributes

Omens of significant change, family and community ties, the ability to see through illusions, exploring the unknown, and symbols of shamanic death and rebirth.

Chakra Interpretations

Root

While caves are where most bats are thought to live, they have adapted to living anywhere they have access to water and a dark place to sleep. For you to be able to sleep well, you probably need it really dark. It could be that you need blackout drapes in your bedroom and may even need to wear an eye mask when you sleep. Most bats live in large communities and have strong family ties. Like the bat, you can live pretty much anywhere; what matters to you is that you are not living alone. If you feel like you have been too solitary, send out your sonar and locate your kindred souls. It's not beneficial for you to be alone.

Sacral

A bat's time is twilight, the classic hour of mystery. As soon as the sun sets, you come alive, so use it to your best advantage. Go into the studio, sit down and write, or spend time touching your lover. Whatever drives your passion, twilight is your most potent time to express it. If you have been contemplating significant changes in your life, the bat is a traditional symbol of shamanic death and rebirth: the breaking down of the old self, old ego, and facing your fears. With the bat as your ally, you will find the wisdom, courage, and perspective to make those changes. Drop down from the safety of your roost, rebirth your new identity, and fly!

Solar Plexus

Unlike birds, bats cannot take off from a standing position; they must drop a few feet before they can fly. It is very likely that the way you express your power is by very unconventional means. Your approach to things may seem difficult or even dangerous to an outside observer, but you trust your inner knowing without question. However, even a bat uses caution, so heed it when the situation calls for it. The majority of the world's bats consume insects, particularly mosquitoes, making them one of nature's best pest control experts. This aspect of the bat could be saying that you tend to be the kind of person who takes care of problems most people find either annoying or disgusting as part of your nature. Doing so feeds a need within you.

Heart

Bats are very affectionate and need the closeness and reassurance of touch. While it may not seem that way to others, your heart needs to touch and be touched. You have a nurturing spirit and use touch as part of communicating and healing. If you are in a field where physical contact is part of your life's work, the bat can be an excellent ally. At the same time, it is possible you are overly empathetic to the feelings of others. If this is the case, keep your shields up so you are protecting your heart.

Throat

One adage says that someone is acting "like an old bat" when they nag too much. Is it possible that you need to use some restraint with your vocalizations? Alternatively, bats have the best hearing of all land mammals. This aspect of the bat could mean that you can hear what others are trying to keep hidden. A third possible similarity is that you are a member of a large family—be it family of origin or family of choice—and you are used to everyone talking at once. Just like a human mother can differentiate her child's voice from all the other children in a playground, a mother bat can differentiate the sound of her pup from the millions of other bats in the cave. You can easily keep up with the cacophony of simultaneous conversations, and you wouldn't want it any other way.

Third Eye

When most of the world is coming inside to find shelter, the bat is at its best. Twilight could be a powerful time for you to do trance work or meditation. Like a bat using echolocation, if you send out a psychic inquiry, an answer will bounce back. While roosting, bats hang upside down, like the Hanged Man in the tarot. This lesson teaches that sometimes you need to look at a situation from a different perspective to truly see it.

Crown

The fact that a bat hangs upside down while it sleeps means that its crown chakra is facing the earth; this is an excellent reminder to stay grounded while meditating. One possibility for you could be some form of inversion meditation. Most bats live in caves filled with the sound of echoes, so if it isn't already part of your meditative practice, you may want to consider using tools of vibrational sound, such as a singing bowl, to connect with this upper chakra. If you do spiritual work with a group, you could try group astral projection and meditation to see if you can meet up on the astral plane.

BEAR

Bears are members of the Ursidae family, whose name comes from Latin *ursus/ursa,* which is also where we get the names Ursa Major (great bear) and Ursa Minor (little bear) in our constellations. Some believe that the bear was one of the first animals to be idolized by humans. Early cave paintings show that ancient humans had a reverence for cave bears, and some prehistoric peoples thought that a bear was the spirit of an ancestor. During the Middle Ages, an excavated skull of a cave bear was thought to be that of a dragon. Bears are extremely intelligent and possess excellent memories. They are known to use tools for both hunting and play, and the black bear has navigational skills far superior to those of humans. The bear is the epitome of the protective mother, primal power, connection with ancestral roots, introspection, and the ability to call on one's inner stores when needed.

Key Attributes

Strength, courage, healing abilities, motherhood, introspection, dreaming, and transformation.

Chakra Interpretations

Root

Bear embodies the regenerative power of hibernation. If you are a man, you might get a lot of benefit from having a "man cave," someplace you can go and be yourself. If you are a woman, you might want to consider a "she den." I created one using a backyard garden shed. Regardless of your gender, you need a private place you can go to recharge. It is also likely that you are quieter during winter months, keeping to yourself and staying home quite a bit, but your energy wakes back up in the spring.

Sacral

Bear being a solitary creature means most likely you keep your desires and your passions to yourself. You may be the kind of person who is happiest working alone in the office, in your studio if you are an artist or musician, or in a workshop if you are a craftsperson of any kind. Bear symbolizes strength, courage, confidence, and standing up to adversity. You have a deep ethical center and clear emotional boundaries. Something to watch for is if this chakra is out of balance, then your inner bear can manifest as an explosive temper.

Solar Plexus

Most people consider bears to be big, ferocious, and scary, but bears are actually shy, solitary creatures and quite docile. They only become aggressive when threatened or if approached when their babies are close. How do you present yourself to the world? Do people find you scary or are you a soft teddy bear? First impressions mean a lot, and when most people see a bear, their first instinct is fear. Bear is teaching you the importance of appearance. Do you want people to be frightened of you, and if they are, would you like them to see the cuddly side as well? It's okay to be a little bit of both; you just need to decide what you want people to see and present it outwardly.

Heart

You have a huge heart! You love with all your soul and can be counted on to give a hug when it's needed or to inspire fear in anyone who threatens to harm someone you love. Bears will risk their own life and even fight to the death to save a cub or sibling from danger. Bear cubs are playful, just like human children; and just like human mothers, if things get too rough, mother bears will make the cubs stop to protect them from hurting each other. Most likely, you are fiercely protective of your children. Children in this sense could be biological children, your animal companions, or even a creative or work project. If you have suffered a loss, climbing into your bear cave to heal is understandable—just try not to stay there too long.

Throat

The bear's diverse forms of communication include body language, vocalizations, and even scents. With a bear in this chakra, you probably need to be aware of your body language when you are speaking, be it in public or to someone for whom you care. If you are physically larger than the person you are having a conversation with, unless you intend to be scary and dominating, try sitting down or crouching so you are at eye level. You'll be less intimidating that way. Bear energy shows that you speak with authority: when you talk, others listen. Just be sure you are aware when your voice is becoming a growl.

Third Eye

Unlike most mammals, bears can see color. They also have a strong sense of smell, even stronger than a dog's. You are probably extremely aware of your surroundings at all times. You may even be clairalient, able to pick up psychic impressions via scent. If there is ever a time when you're sure you smell something that triggers a memory of a loved one who has crossed over, this may be their way of getting your attention. You may not know that you have this gift—it is nothing to fear. Another possible similarity relates to the bear's iconic hibernation. It could mean that sleeping is one of your favorite pastimes. A perfect vacation for you may very well be one where you don't have to go anywhere and can just sleep in for a week.

Crown

Connected to bear's love of sleep, you may be very good at deep trance work or lucid dreaming. Both would come as natural as breathing to you. If you want to connect with your highest self, simply spend time in isolation and quiet contemplation. If you have been feeling like you need to regenerate, consider using your vacation time to participate in a spiritual retreat. No matter how robust you think you are, even a bear gets tired and needs rest and recuperation.

BEAVER

Beavers are semiaquatic, mostly nocturnal animals. Iconic symbols of hard work, they will reengineer a landscape as few other animals can. Some Native Americans called the beaver the "sacred center" of the land. A family of beavers will dam a stream that, once flooded, becomes wetlands and home to nearly half the endangered and threatened species in North America. For this reason, many scientists considered them a *keystone species*, meaning the ecosystem and its inhabitants rely on it for support. Beavers may move with an ungainly waddle on land, but they are graceful swimmers and can remain underwater for nearly fifteen minutes without surfacing. A fun fact about beavers is that they have transparent eyelids that function as goggles, helping them see underwater.

Key Attributes

Industriousness, team player, family and social ties, mastery at building, achieving goals through collaboration, and acting on one's dreams.

Chakra Interpretations

Root

In a perfect world, you would probably choose to live in a wooded area, near water, and in a collaborative community. You may dream of building your own house or may have done so already. It could very well be that you are a builder or architect by trade. If this is not what you do for your living, you might enjoy volunteering your time with organizations that build homes for families in need or rebuild homes for people who lost theirs due to a natural disaster. It could be that you, like beavers, spend nearly all your time working, but it is who you are and doesn't seem to affect your health in a negative way. Most likely, you are the kind of person who doesn't vacation well, unless it involves taking time off from your day job so you can build something for fun.

Sacral

The beaver is happiest when it is creating something. Your passion is building something—be it a home, a family, community, or a business—and you do so through your love of teamwork and collaboration. You would do well as an engineer or organizer for a cause. You work well with others and can keep your ego out of it. As mentioned earlier, a beaver will change a landscape in very beneficial ways, so another passion for you could be working as an environmental engineer.

Solar Plexus

The beaver is a reminder that our dreams need definitive action before they can become a reality. Once you set your mind on a goal, you will work until you achieve it. When beavers construct their home, they leave many ways to escape—a good lesson that forethought will keep you from painting yourself into a metaphorical corner. Some wildlife rehabilitators have found beavers to be gentle beings with a sense of humor. You may have been, or currently are, the class (or office) clown. If nothing else, you have no problem laughing at yourself. Another side of the beaver says you may feel self-conscious about how the world sees you. It might be that you don't feel graceful. If this is the case, try visualizing yourself gliding through water as you move. This aspect of beaver energy will help you find your grace.

Heart

Beavers are monogamous, mate for life, and live in multigenerational communities. Your partner, children, and extended family are what fill your heart. To you, a family doesn't necessarily mean "human"; it can also mean animal companions. Your work environment is where you can be your most authentic self, but only if you are a member of a collaborative team that works to make the world a better place. As mentioned above, if your work environment does not offer you fulfillment, find a place where you can use your skills as a volunteer.

Throat

Beavers are watchful and protective of their lodge-mates. If one of them senses danger, it will use its tail to slap a warning to the invader and raise the alarm. The beaver in this chakra could be saying that while you may not speak out very often, when you do, it is for a good cause. Given the beaver's combined need to be a team player and a builder, you would do well working as a mediator or teaching groups how to work together to build something meaningful. It could also mean something as grounded and practical as teaching shop classes in high schools or volunteering to train unemployed workers new skills.

Third Eye

As mentioned earlier, beavers have transparent eyelids that function as goggles, helping them see underwater. If you tap into this trait, you might be able to glimpse into other realms, worlds, and dimensions that most people can't. You can also use it as a shield to filter out any negativity that might try to creep in. Another possible interpretation is that you tend to look at the world through the proverbial rose-colored glasses. If that is the case, it will benefit you to try clarity. From a practical perspective, if you have a family history of cataracts, it will be wise for you to visit an eye doctor on a regular basis, especially as you get older.

Crown

The beaver in this chakra is an acknowledgment that you prefer working with others in a spiritual or magical community, one with strong ties and that perhaps is even multigenerational. If you aren't already working with a group like this, you would find a lot of benefit in seeking one out. If you are fortunate enough to have a spiritual family already, it is with this family that you are regularly able to tap into something greater than yourself. If your group doesn't already have one, try building a dream lodge together so you can meet up on the astral plane.

BEE

The honey bee has been around for millions of years and is the only insect that produces food eaten by humans. In some cultures, honey has been used as medicine for over five thousand years, and modern medicine is finding uses for it, especially in wound care and cough suppression. Honey contains many of the substances necessary to sustain life, including enzymes, vitamins, minerals, and water, and it also contains an antioxidant associated with improved brain functioning. There are three castes of bee: queen, worker, and drone. All drones are male, all workers are female, and all of them work for one queen. Beyond making honey, bees play a critical role in the delicate balance of our ecosystem. If this small but essential being disappears from our world, humans will not be far behind.

Key Attributes

Fertility, productivity, achieving goals, accomplishing the seemingly impossible, and enjoying the sweetness of life.

Chakra Interpretations

Root

Honey bees have incredible olfactory abilities that aid them in family recognition, social communication within the hive, and odor recognition for finding food. Each beehive has a distinct odor, and bees whose odors do not match will not be allowed in. It could be that you are very sensitive to odors, possibly even suffering from hyperosmia to the point where being around strong odors gives you a headache or makes you feel ill. Opposite of this could be that you love to fill your home with pleasing scents: fresh flowers, scented candles, or even plug-in room fresheners.

Sacral

A bee is hardwired to do specific tasks; they are what it lives for and what gives it pleasure. It is very likely that your job takes up all your waking hours, and you're perfectly okay with that. The mere fact that bees can fly given their size compared to the fragility of their wings is proof that anything is possible with energy and intention. Believe in your abilities, and you can accomplish anything. Stop letting things weigh you down; trust that your wings will lift you. From a practical standpoint, the bee in this chakra could mean that you are a passionate beekeeper.

Solar Plexus

A worker bee's role changes over time as the bee ages. Hive roles include cleaners, undertakers, nurses, builders, temperature controllers, guards, and foragers. When it is clear to you what your role is in the "hive," you give it all your energy. It could be that you have changed careers several times during your lifetime because whatever it was you were doing no longer gave you satisfaction. Maybe you switched majors in school or went back to school after one career had run its course. Another possibility is that you tend to pick a new talent or hobby to explore every few years and then move on to the next thing that strikes your fancy once you feel like you've mastered the last one. A word of caution from the bee in this chakra: a bee will work itself to death, so you might want to ask yourself if it is time to take a vacation.

Heart

In addition to dance, one of the ways bees communicate is by touching each other using their highly sensitive antennae. It is second nature for you to make physical contact with people when you talk. You may not feel like you are connecting with someone unless you do. Researchers believe that some bees are shyer than others and that some are more adventurous. Does either of these aspects speak to you? Are you afraid to reach out for fear of being stung, or can you comfortably do something for the sheer adventure of it? One aspect of bee will speak to a limited number of people: you might lean toward polyamory as a lifestyle, flitting from flower to flower rather than staying with one. If this is the case, just be sure that all parties are agreeable, or someone will be stung.

Throat

Bees don't have ears, but they can still sense sound: they pick up vibrations in the air. From a practical standpoint, perhaps you have trouble with your hearing or may suffer from tinnitus. One aspect of the bee could be a warning to watch how you speak, because your words can be interpreted as both sweetness or stinging. Another trait of the bee is that in addition to touching, bees communicate by dancing. Maybe you need to join a dance class or share a slow romantic dance with your honey.

Third Eye

While most humans see color in combinations of red, blue, and green, bees see colors based on the ultraviolet spectrum in shades of blue and green. From a real-life standpoint, the bee in this chakra could just mean that you live with color vision deficiency, also called color blindness, and you see the world in a different way than most. The fact that bees see ultraviolet light patterns that are invisible to humans can be a useful tool for anyone; it means you can work with the bee to open your mind's eye to see in a different way and in a different spectrum.

Crown

Some think that bees have mathematician-style problem-solving skills. If they have ten flowers to visit, they will work out the shortest route between all of them. The bee in this chakra could very well mean that your mind solves problems faster than most can even start to understand them. You solve complex puzzles seemingly out of thin air. When planning a trip, you most likely know the fastest route and have a plan for any emergencies that may happen along the way. It is possible that your mind is always busy to the point where you are not able to relax enough to connect with this chakra. As mentioned earlier, a bee will work itself to death, so this is a caution that it may be time for you to slow down and smell the roses.

BUFFALO

These majestic beasts are the largest animals found in North America. The buffalo played an essential role in shaping the ecology of the American West. Their hooves loosened the ground, to the benefit of many plant species, and those plants in turn were eaten by many other species. The Plains Indians used every part of the buffalo to help them survive: dung for fuel; hides for clothing, blankets, and shelters; meat for food; and bones for tools and toys. Horns were used to make cups and spoons, and even the tendons were used to make thread for sewing and strings for bows. In many myths, the buffalo sacrificed itself willingly and was therefore treated with honor and respect. In 2016 the buffalo became the national mammal of the United States.

Key Attributes

Walking a sacred path, abundance and gratitude, feminine courage, deep connections with the earth, and strength of character.

Chakra Interpretations

Root

Roaming the land in populations that numbered in the millions, the buffalo were once considered a symbol of the Great Plains. When we think about a buffalo, we rarely think of a singular individual; we think of them in the context of a herd. Most likely, you feel safest when you are in a crowd, even if it is only a few people, and probably one consisting of members of your same gender. It goes against your nature to spend any time alone. Another possibility for the buffalo in this chakra is that you have respect for all things, a gift for sharing, and an instinct to protect, defend, and honor all life. You might be an avid recycler, trying your best not to waste anything or take anything for granted.

Sacral

Female buffalo lead the family groups, while bulls remain solitary or in small groups for most of the year. As mentioned above, you probably tend to spend most of your time amongst members of your same gender. When males and females do come together, the bull will become very possessive of the female he has chosen, even blocking the female's view of competing bulls and bellowing at any male trying to get her attention. It is possible that when you are in a relationship, you become very possessive of your partner, to the point of getting angry if someone so much as looks at them. If this is the case for you, it may be time to search inside yourself to discover the source of the insecurity that makes you need to possess another person. If you are in a relationship in which your partner behaves this way, are you sure you want to stay?

Solar Plexus

The buffalo's massive shoulders are capable of carrying large amounts of weight. This message says that you are willing to take on a great deal, including other people's burdens. Just be sure that the burdens you carry are ones you carry by choice. Buffalo energy is a gentle reminder that it is not your job to take on the weight of the world. Another aspect of the buffalo in this chakra speaks to your awareness that we are all part of a greater whole. While you often stand out in a crowd, you understand that *real* strength comes from connection—to others, to the environment, and to all life.

Heart

When protecting the herd against danger, the females will form a defensive circle around the calves, and the males will form an outer circle around the females. You have a strong character and a protective nature that you use for the benefit of any who need it, particularly those you consider vulnerable. The buffalo is also a reminder that all things are interconnected and that it is not necessary to struggle to have abundance; true abundance is in the heart, not in *things*. It is important to have gratitude for what you have and not worry about the things you don't.

Throat

One way a buffalo communicates is with its tail. If a buffalo is calm, its tail will be hanging straight down and swishing, but an upset buffalo will point its tail upward. Most likely, people can read your moods like a book based on your body language, so you may want to be conscious of what you are projecting. The buffalo in this chakra could also be telling you to use your voice for prayer, for honoring life, or for teaching the young. Your voice can be a tool of the sacred if used with intent. One surprising study showed that when males court a female, the quieter male seems to be the one to win her heart—a lesson that it isn't always the loudest voice that wins, and a reminder to not use your overwhelming presence as your only form of communication.

Third Eye

Buffalo are nearsighted, which could mean you tend to be a little bullheaded when it comes to expanding your awareness beyond what is right in front of you. To compensate for their vision, buffalo have strong senses of smell and hearing. To open this chakra, it may be useful for you to use aromatherapy or essential oils, particularly something with an earthy aroma. Another way could be using music or nature soundtracks. Key here is to not rely on your visual senses.

Crown

Buffalo is a uniting force between things earthly and unearthly. Buffalo is asking you to feel your connection between the Earth Mother and Sky Father. The Lakota legend of White Buffalo Woman teaches that the earth and everything on her are sacred. The buffalo reminds you to be thankful for all that you have and that only by being humble will your relationship with Spirit stay pure. The buffalo represents walking a sacred path and honoring all life. Walking with the buffalo is a prayer. If you are willing to be open to the sacred, the buffalo will help you establish a connection with all that is and help you feel in harmony with all beings of the earth, particularly those that are endangered or threatened.

BUTTERFLY

Scientists estimate there are roughly twenty thousand species of butterflies found on every continent in the world except Antarctica. Images of butterflies have been found in Egyptian frescoes that date back thousands of years. A butterfly's life cycle is made up of four parts, which is the reason it is considered a sign of transformation, rebirth, shape-shifting, and reinventing oneself. Like bees, butterflies are very connected to the earth and susceptible to environmental changes: even small changes can be harmful to the population. One indicator of a healthy ecosystem is the presence of a large number of butterflies. In the folklore of some Native American tribes the butterfly represents change, in others short-lived beauty, and in still others conceit and thoughtless behavior. To some, the butterfly is a messenger from the spirit world. The meaning of that message is dependent on the color of the butterfly, and if a butterfly lands on your shoulder, it is there to bring you comfort.

Key Attributes

Powerful personal transformation, lightness of being, playfulness, joy, creative freedom, and a reminder to not take things too seriously.

Chakra Interpretations

Root

Even though the butterfly is a creature of the air, it is very connected to the earth and its environment. Most likely, you like to surround yourself with color and beauty. The sense of smell is connected to this chakra. You might fill your house with flowers or at least the scent of flowers. You may love gardening as either an actual career or just have an amazing green thumb. You are also very sensitive to your personal living space, and if that seems to become corrupted or uncomfortable and you can't fix the problem, you have no problem moving on to a more peaceful place.

Sacral

When a butterfly emerges from its chrysalis, it must wait to be sure its wings are dry before taking flight. You are a patient person; you don't take any quick action when it comes to life situations until you are confident that the timing is right. If you are in the midst of significant change in your life or if you have been feeling like you are in need of change, what stage of transformation are you in, and is anything keeping you from completing the cycle? One habit of the butterfly is flitting from pretty flower to pretty flower. While this will only speak to a few, if it rings true for you, it is likely that you usually don't stay with one partner for very long.

Solar Plexus

It may come as a surprise, but underneath the tiny colorful scales, butterfly wings are transparent. Nearly every species of butterfly is beautiful. Can you see your inner beauty clearly or do you depend on external color—be it makeup or a business suit—to feel safe in the world? Are you afraid of what others will think of you once you strip off your filters? It is also possible that these filters are what give you strength and that you love to parade your colors. What is important is for you to be true to yourself.

Heart

Butterflies are very fragile and easily hurt. If you have suffered a loss or feel like your wings are damaged, it may be healing for you to cocoon yourself for a time so that you can come back into the world transformed and beautiful. Another notable aspect of the butterfly is that it can have a flighty nature. Like the bee, the butterfly is easily distracted by the next pretty flower. As with the sacral, the butterfly in the heart chakra may indicate that you get bored easily and tend to not stay in a relationship long enough to get to know the other person. If this is true for you, could it be time to try settling down?

Throat

Butterflies can't hear, but their wings are very sensitive, and they can feel the vibrations different sounds make. Since the butterfly experiences sound instead of hearing it, you probably are very empathetic to the feelings behind someone's words, getting the real intention. From a real-life standpoint, it could be that you have difficulty with your hearing and need to depend on reading either lips or a person's body language for clarity.

Third Eye

Butterflies have compound eyes made up of thousands of smaller eyes called *ommatidia*. When the butterfly's brain combines the images from these eyes, they become a whole picture—much like many pixels coming together to create a digital image. You not only have the ability to see the pieces of a situation, but you can also put together the whole picture. The butterfly's field of vision is larger than a human's, and it can see both ultraviolet and polarized light. The ability to see in a different wavelength suggests you could have an aptitude for clairvoyant skills. It is highly likely that you are naturally psychic and may even be able to see the veil between the worlds.

Crown

A butterfly's antennae are crucial to its survival. They are used not only for navigation but also for finding food and even for knowing what time of day it is. If their antennae get damaged, they lose these abilities. This speaks to the importance of not breaking your connection to the land or Spirit. Keeping those connections is an essential element in maintaining a balanced life. As mentioned above, butterflies can see both ultraviolet and polarized light. You have an inborn ability to journey into these higher realms of consciousness. Travel there and reconnect with beauty. The Blackfoot tribe believes that dreams are brought in sleep by a butterfly. Perhaps the butterfly has a dream for you if you are open to the message.

CAT

Some believe that the cat is the only animal to domesticate itself voluntarily. It was thought that cats lived first with ancient Egyptians, but the oldest known pet cat was found in a 9,500-year-old grave on the Mediterranean island of Cyprus, predating the Egyptians by thousands of years. Black cats are considered good luck in Britain and Australia (and to anyone who lives with them), but in many parts of Europe and North America, they are feared. The sad reality for black cats in the United States is that they are very often targeted for abuse or torture and are some of the hardest to place from a shelter, especially if they are adult or senior cats.

Key Attributes

Independence, cleverness, curiosity, love of mystery, dignity, sensuality, recognition of multiple lives, being secretive, and patience before action.

Chakra Interpretations

Root

Your needs are basic: a safe place to sleep and food, though you probably prefer that someone else feed you. Most likely, you are a creature of habit and don't like change, particularly to your eating schedule. You want events to occur at the same time and in the same way every day. Your internal clock is uncanny, especially when your stomach is involved. It's okay to be this rigid in your patterns—just don't hiss at people when things don't go your way. Cats are typically the epitome of what it means to be grounded. If you have been working too hard, take a tip from cat and give yourself a break to take a nap in the sun. On the other side of this, if you have become lazy and are just lying around doing nothing, it may be time to wake up. Sometimes life events that are out of our control—illness, being out of work, or even depression—can bring this behavior on. If this is the case, try to keep your mind active or seek outside or professional help if necessary.

Sacral

Cats are extremely independent and at the same time can be very demanding. You might go from being very affectionate to wanting to be left alone in the blink of an eye. You are perfectly fine pursuing whatever it is that pleases you as a solitary, but you also like your playtime with others, provided it is on your terms. Your curiosity knows no bounds, and sometimes that can get you into trouble. Since cats spend most of their time sleeping, most likely your bedroom is your sanctuary. You may also be the kind of person who needs to take regenerative naps before your creativity flows.

Solar Plexus

A cat's whiskers are touch receptors, which gives it a heightened sense of feeling and helps it detect changes in its surroundings. Your instincts are highly tuned, and you tend to sense what others miss. A downside to this is that you might become a scaredy-cat, afraid of everything that lurks in the shadows. Cats have intense focus. When you undertake a task, you do so without distraction. Courageous cats project mystery. You are capable of being invisible or seen depending on your mood or intention. Like a cat, you probably carry yourself with grace, confidence, and pride, without ever realizing you're doing it.

Heart

People who don't live with cats usually are not aware of how affectionate they are and how demanding of love they can be. The cat in this chakra could be telling you that you need to work on balancing your need for personal space with spending time with others. Make sure those you care about know how you feel about them; don't keep it a secret. I do, however, recommend that you don't show that affection by bringing home dead things—unless of course you are a hunter or someone who likes to fish, and it is food for the table!

Throat

A cat's meow is not natural cat language—cats seemed to have developed it to be able to communicate with humans. What is natural is their purr, which in addition to being a sign of contentment can also be a sign of nervousness and a form of self-healing. Some believe that when a human is sick, their companion cat will lie on or next to them and purr, trying to help them heal. (Mine did.) How do you communicate with people? Do you tend to hiss most of the time? Do you need to purr more? There are many forms of sound healing within the spiritual community, but the cat in this chakra also means that you would work well as a counselor or therapist by using your voice to help people heal.

Third Eye

A cat's night vision is impressive. Cats can see in light levels much lower than those needed by a human. You probably don't have any trouble driving at night, a good thing if you drive for a living or tend to work nights. Even though cats have excellent vision, they are unable to focus on anything less than a foot from them. As observant as you can be, be careful not to miss the obvious. Quietly observant, cats can seem to be asleep and ignoring their surroundings, but they are listening to and are aware of everything going on around them. You may be one of those lucky people who can sleep anywhere no matter how chaotic the surrounding area and still know what had been going on when you wake up.

Crown

If you watch cats sleep, you can see their eyelids twitch, and some will make chattering noises and move their paws as if chasing something. It is likely that you are gifted with lucid dreaming. Cats, by nature, are profoundly psychic and seem to sense dimensions that humans can't. Because it is believed they can see in the UV spectrum, it could be that they are able to see auras and possibly even the spirit world. Perhaps you can already see auras or other realms, but if not, try opening your mind using cat sense. You might be surprised.

COYOTE

This member of the dog family once lived primarily in open prairies and deserts but can now be found over most of North America and has even adapted to life in cities. The coyote appears in several Native American tales as a very intelligent trickster. Like the wolf, the coyote mates for life and has strong family ties. Within a pack, the alpha pair will mate, and subordinates usually help raise the young. Coyote energy is often linked to simplicity and trust, reminding us that having a childlike innocence can be a wonderful way to approach the world.

Key Attributes

Deep family connections; understanding that all life is sacred; cleverness; ability to laugh at oneself; learning from mistakes; adaptability; and having a playful, childlike wisdom and innocence.

Chakra Interpretations

Root

Coyote energy says you adapt quickly to new situations. You may love a good joke and find joy in everything you do. It is possible that you have a very close-knit family, be it family of origin or family of choice, and probably work well with children. Because coyotes are members of the Canidae family, most people think they are primarily meat eaters, but coyotes will eat pretty much anything they can find. A word of caution for you: be careful what you eat and make sure it isn't always garbage.

Sacral

Coyotes are active mostly during the night or early in the morning just before dawn. From a practical standpoint, this could be when your thoughts are at their clearest and when you can be at your most productive. Coyote energy is a reminder that it is important to be wise but to also be passionate and foolish, bringing out your trickster side. One caution is to be careful not to become a victim of your foolishness and tricks. Just like their domestic cousins, coyotes love to play. While it is essential to spend a good bit of your waking hours working for your survival, it is equally important to remember to frolic. You might gain a fresh perspective.

Solar Plexus

Coyotes sometimes walk on their toes, so they make very little noise. This trick helps keep them from being detected by predators. It is possible that you feel the need to walk around on eggshells or camouflage yourself, preferring to stay hidden, only revealing yourself to those you consider to be part of your pack. Most coyotes are shy and will flee to safe distance rather than face a confrontation. You might be the kind of person who hides their fear with humor and jokes. Is it time for you to give a warning bark instead? Another side of coyote energy is asking if your trickster nature has you going from one disaster to the next. If so, are you willing to take responsibility for your actions, and do you learn from your mistakes or keep repeating them?

Heart

Coyotes mate for life and they have close family ties, especially when children are involved. You will often go to extremes to protect and nurture family members. A coyote can tell the emotions and mood of fellow pack members by reading facial expressions and body language. Your empathy shows itself with those in your inner circle. No matter what someone may say, you always can tell how they feel by how they carry themselves and other nonverbal clues they give.

Throat

Coyotes are often called *song dogs* because they sing to keep track of pack members and to communicate with other families. Like the wolf, each coyote has a unique voice that can be recognized by those family members, even over long distances. Coyote in this chakra is asking you how long it has been since you heard a friendly voice or talked to someone you care about who lives far away. Perhaps conflicting schedules keep you from seeing each other on a regular basis. It might be time to stop emailing or texting and pick up the phone. Nothing replaces the actual voice of someone you love. The person you call may need that contact as much as you do.

Third Eye

As mentioned earlier, a coyote's time is late evening or early morning. While this is a perfect time for you to get work done, it may be hard for you to relax or meditate during these hours. Another aspect relates to the coyote's keen observational skills. There probably isn't much that escapes your notice, even if you don't say anything. The coyote is telling you to trust your intuition; you are rarely wrong.

Crown

In addition to the trickster, coyote energy represents the magic of life and creation and is a reminder that you don't have to be serious all the time. It's hard to connect with Spirit if you have forgotten how to laugh. Wisdom and folly are two sides of the same coin, and only by understanding that can you find balance within. Many studies have shown that laughter can be a healing tool. Maybe it is time for you to take a breath, let go, and have a good laugh, even if what you're laughing at is yourself.

CROW

These brilliant members of the genus *Corvus* are resourceful tool makers and have amazing problem-solving skills. They have excellent memories and can recognize faces. When they see a person they think has been mean to them, they will teach other crows how to identify that individual and have even been known to drop stones or sticks on the person. On the other side of this, crows have been known to leave gifts for humans they like. Crows tend to live in multigenerational family groups and are always on guard for threats to their home territory and quick to alert the rest of the group to dangers. Crows are very emotional creatures and even mourn their dead. They have been witnessed having what is thought to be a funeral; however, some researchers believe it is more likely that they are trying to figure out what happened and to determine if it posed any threat to the members of the flock. Think of it as *CSI: Crow*.

Key Attributes

Keepers of sacred law, an omen of change, intelligence, transcendence, intuition, dreaming, magic, empathy, speaking your truth, achieving goals with determination and creative thinking, strong ties to community, and knowing your life's mission.

Chakra Interpretations

Root

We usually associate crows with making a lot of noise, but where they nest needs to be a quiet, well-hidden shelter away from predators and bad weather. You might be the kind of person who is okay going into a city or noisy office to work, but you need to come home to a quiet location. Some crows leave the nest once they become an adult, but many choose to stay and live cooperatively, helping raise and defend the young. These family groups often contain members from multiple generations. This speaks to the importance of family to you, including your extended family—grandparents, aunts, uncles, and cousins. If you aren't close to your family of origin, finding a family of choice that crosses many generations can be equally beneficial for you. Simply put, you don't have to, nor should you, go it alone.

Sacral

When you see a group of crows, it is nearly impossible to distinguish one from the other. Standing out in a crowd is not important to you. In fact, it gives you a lot of emotional security and you probably feel safest when you blend in with your peers. Another trait of the crow is that it seems to play for the sheer joy of it. Since crows are tool makers, you might get a lot of entertainment out of figuring out puzzles, inventing something that has practical uses, or even craft making. Crows are fearless, so working with crow energy can help you act with forethought, intent, and confidence.

Solar Plexus

When crow sets itself to a task, it doesn't stop until the task is done, no matter how many attempts or how many times it needs to change tactics. You are known for seeing a project through to its completion. When you start a project or a task, you probably know the outcome in your mind before you even get started. In fact, having a vision of the project might be the trigger that gets you started—just remember to take it one step at a time. This is a lesson for you to trust your gut instincts, to think for yourself and not follow the crowd. You might just come up with something the world has never seen.

Heart

Crows are incredibly emotional. They express feeling with displays of happiness, anger, sadness, and even grief. You may be someone who wears their heart on their sleeve. People close to you can tell right away what kind of mood you are in; at the same time, you can read them just as easily. A mated pair of crows will often remain together for life, so your preference would be to find a life mate. Crow energy guides the magic of shape-shifting. If some darkness from your past is keeping your heart from loving, it may be time for you to reshape your heart and allow love to enter.

Throat

Crows have a very sophisticated and distinctive form of language, and their caw has a different meaning at different times. They have been known to mimic sounds of not only humans but also other animals and can associate noises with events. You might enjoy entertaining your friends by imitating their voices or those of celebrities. While crows aren't known for having beautiful voices, they are still considered songbirds. You may not think you have a very nice voice, but that shouldn't stop you from singing if it brings you joy. Another possibility is that you are one to speak out for others. You would do well using your voice to teach or defending what you feel is a just cause.

Third Eye

As with most nesting birds, crows are born with their eyes closed but open them after just a few days. From a spiritual or intuitive perspective, you may have spent your early years with blinders on, refusing to or not being allowed to see anything but the tangible. Perhaps you still have those blinders on. Align with crow energy to expand your self-knowledge beyond two-dimensional vision. While most of us humans see three primary colors, crows see four, and they can spot things from long distances with pinpoint precision. It is possible that you observe things, whether on the physical or ethereal plain, with an accuracy that others do not. If this is the case, honor it, and know that it is your gift.

Crown

In some traditions, the crow is the bringer of messages from the spirit world. It dwells beyond the realm of time and space. In sunlight, a crow's black feathers show the violet iridescence of this chakra. Crow energy can be your guide to the higher realms and a reminder that all life is sacred and magical. Crow in this chakra can be a message that if you are doing solitary spiritual work, it may be time to find a group. A crow is at its best when it is with family.

DEER

The deer belongs to a family called Cervidae that includes the caribou, the elk, and the moose. They live in many different habitats, including tundra, tropical rainforests, and woodland—anywhere that has plenty of food and places to hide. Deer are beautiful creatures that can run very fast and jump over high obstacles. Throughout time, man has hunted deer, using their meat for food, their hides for clothing, and their antlers for weapons. Deer have appeared in art from the time of cave paintings to the present and have even played a role in heraldry, religion, and literature. The animal's appearance in mythology extends worldwide, appearing in Egyptian, Greek, Native American, and Celtic legend. For purposes of *Chakra Animals*, I focus on the female deer. The male deer, the stag (see page 150), has entirely different interpretations.

Key Attributes

Sensitivity, intuition, gentleness, dignity, facing challenges and fears with grace, living from the heart, unconditional love, kindness, gratitude, and honoring the sacred.

Chakra Interpretations

Root

A mother deer will leave her newborn fawns in a safe hiding place while she goes out in search of food. Young fawns aren't yet able to keep up with mommy while she forages for food, so at dawn she leaves them in a safe place to wait for her return at dusk. Many human families face a similar challenge. They need to leave their children either with a relative or in daycare while they go off to work for the survival of the household. Most likely your job is merely a means of survival, and you look forward to the end of the day when you can be home again with your spouse or partner, your housemates, your children, your companion animals, or even your garden.

Sacral

By observing deer, you can learn the gift of gentleness. Deer can hide in plain sight by being perfectly still while remaining fully alert to their surroundings. Regardless of your gender, deer energy speaks to the feminine aspects within. Deer teaches that caring and gentleness, often toward yourself, can help you overcome stressful situations. It may be time for you to stop being so hard on yourself and treat yourself with more kindness.

Solar Plexus

Deer energy has gentle courage and is not afraid to face internal demons. If you are in a situation, be it at work, home, or school, where you are being terrorized by another, standing up to the person with courage and gentleness and not stooping to their level of behavior may help confuse them enough that they get bored and move on. If not, use the deer's ability to run and leap to find cover: remove yourself from the situation or seek outside help. Another possibility is the deer may be telling you that you are fearful of your own power. If this is the case, it may be time to call on the male aspect of the stag to help you.

Heart

The deer is a gentle, graceful creature full of subtlety, elegance, and unconditional love. Deer's energy can see the wounds within another's soul and will help heal it with gentleness and compassion. You can tell when someone is in pain, and you are called from your core to help them heal with compassion. You might do well in grief counseling, as a minister of some sort, or even working in a hospice setting. The deer's message for the heart is that we should move through life with pure intention. Only with love, both for ourselves and for others, can we understand the true meaning of wholeness.

Throat

People will close their ears to a shout but will bend closer to hear a whisper. You are one who speaks with the gentleness of the deer and understands that you can get your point across more effectively that way than with aggression. Deer have remarkable hearing. They can determine not only where the sound originated but also if it represents a potential danger. Like a deer, you have sensitive hearing and can quickly tell if what you are hearing presents a threat, be it a strange sound or someone else's words.

Third Eye

The white-tailed deer's peripheral vision range is close to 300 degrees, but it doesn't have much in the way of depth perception. Ever on the defensive for predators, they can pick up the slightest movement that is around them, but they can't focus or tell what it is unless it is right in front of them. You see the far-reaching perspective of any situation, and you take it all in before acting or making a comment. The deer in this chakra could also mean that you live your life always on the defensive, looking for danger, even when none is there.

Crown

One of the deer's messages is that when you explore spirituality, you harm none with your actions. You must walk through the world of spirit with love and respect—respect not just for Spirit and the land but for your fellow travelers as well. This is also a reminder for you to be gentle with yourself. Perhaps the deer is calling you to the wild green places so that you can regenerate. Sitting by a stream in the woods may be where you can truly be calm and reflective, drinking in the peace.

DOG

Throughout history, dogs have represented loyalty, protection, companionship, and unconditional love. For thousands of years, humans have been selectively breeding dogs for various behaviors, sensory capabilities, and physical attributes. They range in size from tiny, like the papillon or Yorkie, to huge, like the mastiff or Great Dane. Dogs make excellent service animals, and historical references to them being used for this purpose date as far back as the sixteenth century. The first actual school to train guide dogs opened to help veterans of World War I with disabilities in Germany, but the first organized use of dogs to assist the blind goes back to the 1780s. Dogs are the domestic version of wolves, are equally family oriented, and, like the wolf, follow the lead of the alpha. In your home situation, that can be either a man or a woman, whoever they sense is in charge, and they consider all in the home to be members of the pack, even the cat.

Key Attributes

Loyalty, friendship, empathy, unconditional love, guardianship, trustworthiness, friendship, community, selfless service.

Chakra Interpretations

Root

For a dog to feel safe, it needs a home. The dog in the root chakra is an acknowledgment that you enjoy domestic life and take a lot of pride in defending it. Your inner wolf probably doesn't interest you very much; your priorities are a place to call home, a comfy bed, food on a regular basis, and maybe even a yard to play in. You may also be somewhat territorial, especially when it comes to the people in your life. Just be sure he other humans want your protection, so they don't feel owned by you.

Sacral

Dogs will give of themselves regardless of how they are treated. A dog that hasn't been mistreated and knows its place in the pack has a confident, joyful approach to life. But a dog that has been treated with cruelty can be fearful or mean. Which speaks truth to you? If life events or another person has kicked you a little too much and you want to get your confidence and trust back, call on the dog as an ally. Dogs have very keen instincts about people. When someone approaches you wearing a smile but something just feels wrong, trust your instincts. They will rarely fail you.

Solar Plexus

Worldwide there are well over three hundred species of dog, all with a vast array of temperaments and behaviors. Dogs will eagerly do a task that is in keeping with their nature. For example, retrievers are meant to fetch, herders herd, and guard dogs guard. You wouldn't expect a Yorkie to herd sheep, nor would you expect a border collie to ride around in a purse. It is essential to know and accept who you are and what you can offer to someone so that they know what their expectations of you should be. Be sure that you are being true to your nature and not trying to fit into someone else's idea of you.

Heart

It brings you great joy to be there when someone close to your heart needs you. You are incredibly loyal to all who find their way into your heart. You are the kind of person who drops whatever they are doing to help a friend or family member in need or to come to their defense. Most likely, your warmth and smile can soothe even the darkest pain of another. A word of caution: be sure that your loyalty is not being taken for granted and that you are also being loyal to yourself.

Throat

Dogs have a variety of vocalizations, and most are used as warnings or alarms. When you sense something is wrong, you are usually the first person to speak up and often quite loudly, especially if it is in defense of something or someone you love. Another possible interpretation of the dog in the throat chakra relates to how you communicate with other people. Do you have a habit of growling or barking orders? At the same time, the dog might also be saying that it is time for you to learn how to bark a warning for your own protection.

Third Eye

It is a misconception that dogs see shades of gray instead of color. In reality, their color perception is similar to that of a human with red-green color blindness. The dog in this chakra could just mean that you also see the world in this way. While many dogs are nearsighted, their vision is far more sensitive than ours when it comes to spotting motion from a distance. You might understand the outcome of a situation long before it becomes an issue. Dogs can pick up on subtle energy frequencies that humans often block. So, if this chakra feels blinded, call on the energy of the dog to guide you through the darkness.

Crown

Are you loyal to your highest self and your connection with Spirit? Are you naively giving your trust to a guide or a teacher who claims that only through their leadership can you find the higher realms? Be sure that you don't blindly give your trust. Maybe you are being called to be a guide to lead others out of the darkness. If this is the case for you, you may find it very rewarding as long as you remember to treat them as young pups to be prepared for life and not sheep to be herded.

DOLPHIN

Dolphins are highly intelligent marine mammals who once lived on land, entering the water approximately fifty million years ago. Most researchers agree that dolphins are social beings that depend on collaborative community groups called *pods* for hunting and defense. These groups can range in size, having anywhere from just a few individuals to several hundred members. They often ride the leading wave of boats and will help swimmers in trouble. Because dolphins don't have olfactory lobes or nerves, they probably can't smell.

Key Attributes

Harmony and balance, peace, grace and gentleness, playfulness, joy, intelligence, protection, and a reminder to keep a sense of humor.

Chakra Interpretations

Root

As mentioned above, dolphins live in social groups, and those social relationships tend to be long-lasting, even if the dolphins don't stay with the same group. Like in many mammal friendships, dolphins will remember each other even if it has been years since they last saw each other. Male dolphin buddies may stay together for many decades and might join other pods together. Females group together because they get help raising their young from other female relatives. You are a people person but may find yourself changing social groups every few years. There is nothing wrong with this pattern; for you, the joy is in exploring new waters and meeting new people. At the same time, while you are in each of these new groups, there is probably one or two people whom you remain in contact with or at least catch up with every few years, and when you do, it is as if no time has passed. You just pick up your conversation where you left off.

Sacral

The dolphin has a lot of joyous energy. You probably love to entertain and are the life of the party wherever you go. Your creative juices are probably constantly flowing. A not-so-flattering aspect of dolphin life is that while dolphins seem carefree and playful, they are also extremely sexual. Female dolphins are often the victim of groups of males forcing themselves on her. Given the male dolphins' violent behavior, the female can't say no or change her mind. If the dolphin has shown up in this chakra and the first interpretation doesn't fit, you may need to ask yourself if your passions are controlling you, even to the point of causing harm to another person. It is also possible that you are letting another person harm you. If that is the case, I urge you to seek help.

Solar Plexus

When most people think of dolphins, they think of them as being peaceful, but as with all intelligent mammals, this is not always the case. Some researchers call dolphins "the gangsters of the sea" because they have been observed patrolling in gang-like groups. Each gang includes subgroups that protect the group's females, recruit other members, or act as liaisons to communicate with rival pods. Where are you within the hierarchy in your life? Are you the leader, or are you more comfortable being the peaceful negotiator? Wherever you feel your placement is, be comfortable swimming in your truth.

Heart

In certain legends and old sea tales, there are claims of dolphins helping drowning sailors, rescuing people from sharks, and making themselves useful as guides through dangerous waters. Dolphins will help injured family members and newborn babies by swimming under them and nudging them up to the surface so they can breathe. There have been some reports of them doing the same for humans in trouble. This says that you will go above and beyond to help others. You would do well as a healer, working in emergency services, or as a first responder, saving people.

Throat

Dolphins are master communicators, and each has a whistle that is unique to the individual. Some researchers believe that dolphins name each other and also name things. Similar to how canine species have a distinct voice that is recognized by family members, a dolphin can recognize the voice of a friend or family member. As mentioned for the root chakra, you may go many years without seeing a friend, but you recognize their voice instantly. In addition to vocal abilities, the dolphin's auditory nerve is about three times the size of the human's, allowing them to hear frequencies far beyond human hearing. The combination of these abilities says you communicate your thoughts and intentions clearly but also listen and understand on multiple levels. Your voice can put a smile on the face of someone who needs it.

Third Eye

Dolphins have excellent eyesight that is particularly adapted for seeing underwater. From a practical perspective, it is very possible that you have and will maintain 20/20 eyesight or better throughout most of your life. Similar to bats, dolphins use echolocation to navigate and hunt. This translates to them being very sensitive to subtle vibrations. Dolphin energy shows that you are highly empathetic and receptive. When you are open to these impressions, you typically find that what you "see" turns out to be entirely accurate.

Crown

Like whales and seals, dolphins only allow half their brain to go to sleep, while the other half remains awake so that they can continue to breathe. Your brain may stay active even when you sleep, giving you very vivid dreams, which you recall effortlessly. If it isn't already part of your practice, you should try intentional dreaming. In some spiritual disciplines, the dolphin represents the breath of life, life force, and resurrection. Work with dolphin energy if you are going through a spiritual rebirth or if you just need to remember to relax and breathe.

DOVE

Around the world, there are more than three hundred species of pigeon and dove, and all of them are part of the same family, Columbidae. The main difference between the pigeon and the dove is one of language: *pigeon* is what they were called in France, and *dove* comes from Germany. Doves have long been a favorite subject in art to symbolize the divine, and their interpretation changes depending on the culture and belief system. In the Mediterranean and ancient Near East, the dove was a symbol of the mother goddess. The best-known dove story comes from the Hebrew Bible and the story of Noah. As recently as the nineteenth century, sailors were still using doves and other birds to help them find and navigate toward land. For centuries, they were used to deliver messages, especially during times of war. We often see doves being used as an emblem of peace during battle negotiations or in weddings to symbolize love. The names *dove* and *pigeon* are often used interchangeably, as I do below.

Key Attributes

Peace, love, grace, empathy, the gentleness of spirit, smoothing and healing troubled thoughts, femininity, tranquility, simplicity, and blessings from the Holy Spirit.

Chakra Interpretations

Root

A homing pigeon has the capacity to find its way home over hundreds or even thousands of miles. You probably have an uncanny sense of direction, don't have a use for maps or GPS, and rarely get lost. It might also be possible that you are required to travel quite a bit for your job, and the one thing that keeps you going is the thought of home. No matter how far you roam, be it by choice or at the insistence of another, you always come home to roost.

Sacral

When most birds see a reflection, they think it is a rival for their territory, but doves are capable of self-recognition and understand that they are looking at themselves. The face you present to the world is your real face. You know who you are, and you are comfortable showing the world even any self-perceived flaws you feel you have. What you may not be aware of is that the world sees someone of calm beauty and intelligence. If you experienced trauma in your past, working with dove's energy can help you release any emotional damage trapped in your cellular memory. Try a tonal form of meditation, something that gently vibrates your cells to aid with the release.

Solar Plexus

Doves have a very gregarious nature. They are quite social and are frequently found in flocks of twenty or more birds. When you see a flock of doves, it is hard to distinguish one bird from another. You may take a lot of pride in keeping up with the latest trends, making sure you fit in with your crowd and don't stand out as being different. It could also be that you are quite shy and afraid of expressing your beauty. If this rings true, maybe it's time for you to stop allowing someone else to define what your beauty should be.

Heart

Like 90 percent of all bird species, doves tend to mate for life, and both partners participate in raising their young. Most likely, your preference is to have one partner for life and possibly to have several children together. These children could be biological or adopted. If it isn't human children you want, maybe you and your partner share your home with many companion animals, a fabulous garden, or even a business. Like a dove, you are very good-natured and social and do best with a companion. Your heart is open, peaceful, and loving. You care for everyone you meet, as long as they do you no harm.

Throat

Some scientists believe that one of the reasons for doves' navigational prowess is their ability to hear low-frequency sound waves. You could be clairaudient, or perhaps when someone speaks, you listen carefully for the underlying meaning behind their words. A dove's call can be soothing, but to some it sounds like a sad lament. Most likely, your voice has the magical skill of being able to calm stressful situations and smooth even the most ruffled feathers. You would do well as a peace negotiator or may excel at easing tension in a business meeting.

Third Eye

Doves can see not only color but also the ultraviolet light spectrum. To them, tones are amplified and far brighter than what we perceive. It is possible that you have excellent color perception. It could also be that you tend to look at the bright side of any situation. The dove in this chakra might indicate that your vision has become dimmed by exhaustion. If your mind is too busy, working with dove energy will remind you that peace is always just a breath away. Practicing deep breathing and meditation will help you find peace, quiet your inner chaos, and assist you in seeing the brilliant world around you.

Crown

Throughout time, the dove has been revered by many of the world's religions as a messenger from Spirit. In some cultures, they also represent reincarnation. The dove in this chakra is saying that your channel to Spirit is open, clear, and beautiful. It could also mean that your channel to the other side of the veil is clear as well. However, as mentioned above, if your mind has been too busy to be receptive, try some deep breathing exercises and allow dove's gentle wings to carry you into the divine realms.

DRAGONFLY

Dragonflies were one of the first winged insects to evolve roughly three million years ago and had wingspans that could reach up to two feet. Part of dragonfly's magical appeal is their iridescence, and another is the incredible way they fly. Dragonflies have two pairs of wings that can beat either together or separately, which allows them to turn rapidly in midair, hover, and even fly backward or straight up and down like a helicopter. This amazing skill inspired engineers to try to design robots that can maneuver like them. Dragonflies help ecologists monitor wetland ecosystems because their numbers give an indication about the health of their aquatic habitat. In addition, since they are low on the food chain and prey to several types of creatures, including frogs and birds, studying their numbers can reveal changes in water ecosystems more quickly than studying other species or plants. Scientists also use them to test for the presence of heavy metals.

Key Attributes

Power of light, breaking down illusions, understanding dreams, magic and mysticism, shape-shifting, transformation, joy, and lightness of spirit and being.

Chakra Interpretations

Root

All dragonflies start their life in water and tend to remain within a few miles of the place where they hatched. You probably feel the need to be near water, but what is even more important to you is to live very near the area where you were raised. It is possible that you still live in the house you grew up in or at least in the same neighborhood. Another aspect of dragonfly in the root chakra talks of most species' need to warm up in the sun before they can fly. If this is the case for you, you are probably not a morning person. You perhaps need to wake up slowly and enjoy your tea or coffee while sitting in the morning sun, or at the very least under the light of your desk lamp.

Sacral

Nearly all dragonflies are beautifully iridescent. You like to wear beautiful colors or sparkly jewelry. Many dragonflies change color as they mature. The dragonfly tells you not to fight the changes your body is going through as you age but to be comfortable with the transformation and to revel in it. Another aspect of dragonfly in this chakra speaks to the fact that dragonflies mate while flying. It may be that your sexual activities lean toward the athletic. Or if physical aspects of your relationship have become regular or boring, the dragonfly could be telling you to try something new and different to bring back the magic. Maybe it is time for you and your lover to get away together.

Solar Plexus

Dragonflies don't track their prey. Instead, they can anticipate where it will be and intercept it midflight. You accurately make a plan and only act when you are sure the timing is right. You might be skilled at games of strategy, such as chess. As mentioned earlier, dragonflies have amazing flying ability. This may be an indication that you move through the world in ways that others can't keep up with and that may seem directionless to an outside observer, but you know exactly where you're going. Yet another possibility of dragonfly in the solar plexus chakra is that you have a lot of nervous energy and can be a bit of a diva. You may love to be flashy, and your energetic nature brightens up any room when you make your magical appearance.

Heart

Most of a dragonfly's life is spent underwater in the larval stage as a nymph, and its time as the beautiful adult we see flying around is very short. The dragonfly is a reminder not to take a single moment for granted. Do what is right for your heart. Never assume that there is always tomorrow, and never forget to tell the people you care about how you feel about them. Follow your heart and live life to the fullest now.

Throat

Dragonflies are carnivores and have insatiable appetites. Their diet is mostly pesky insects like mosquitoes, gnats, and flies. This says you can silence anyone that you feel is annoying. Another aspect of the dragonfly is that it catches its food while flying. You probably tend to eat on the run, rarely stopping to take a break to enjoy your meal. This could be a caution that if your life has become chaotic, you need to take a break, or you won't be able to communicate with anyone.

Third Eye

Dragonflies' eyes take up the majority of their heads, allowing them to see in every direction except right behind them. You can see the big picture of most situations and are pretty good at not looking back when it is time to move on. In contradiction to that, the dragonfly in this chakra can be warning you not to be so focused on the future that you forget to remember the lessons of your past, thus doomed to repeat them. Another aspect, as mentioned earlier, of the dragonfly is that it lives most of its life underwater as a nymph. The dragonfly is asking you if it is time for you to reveal your wings and take flight into a new and higher perspective.

Crown

Dragonflies are light-benders. Their iridescent body and wings reflect light and can be interpreted as a call to bring color, magic, and transformation into your life. Try hanging prisms in a sunny window to allow rainbow light to enter your home. You can also use a crystal as a meditation tool, letting natural or candlelight shine through. The dragonfly in this chakra is also a reminder of its flying capabilities. When you are ready to launch yourself into the higher realms, you won't have any limitations in the direction of your flight. Allow the dragonfly's amazing flight ability to carry you to places you didn't think possible.

EAGLE

We all know that birds evolved from dinosaurs. Descending from a seabird called a *kite*, the majestic eagle broke off into its current species roughly thirty-six million years ago. Currently, there are approximately sixty different species of eagle living on every continent except Antarctica, with most residing in Eurasia and Africa. Outside of those geographic areas, nine are found in Central and South America, three in Australia, and two in North America, including the bald and golden eagles. Two species of the Eurasian eagles often "visit" North America by way of the Aleutian Islands and will often nest in Alaska. For purposes of interpretation, I use the bald and golden eagles. Eagles have inspired humans for ages; ancient Greeks associated the eagle with Zeus, the Thunderbird of Native American mythology resembles the eagle, and in Gaelic lore the eagle is associated with the sun. In ancient Aztec tradition, the chief god told his people to settle where they would find an eagle perched on a cactus eating a snake, so they built the great city Tenochtitlan in the area now known as Mexico City. Since 1782, the bald eagle has been the national bird and symbol of the United States.

Key Attributes

Connecting with one's spiritual path, spirit vision, strength, wisdom, knowledge of magic, seeing from a higher perspective, independence, freedom, authority, courage, and achieving one's goals through determination and confidence.

Chakra Interpretations

Root

Most bald eagles live near water because fish is their preferred diet. Golden eagles tend to live around mountains and canyons, and their diet consists primarily of small birds and mammals. What matters to you for your survival will depend on which eagle resonates with you. Do you need to live near water with seafood as your primary diet, or do you prefer a dryer locale with meat being what fills your freezer? What matters is for you to be true to your nature and live and eat in ways that give you strength.

Sacral

Eagles are bigger and more powerfully built than most other birds of prey. In a crowd, you carry yourself with pride. You might even stand out as seeming larger than you are. You approach everything you undertake with passion, dignity, and confidence. However, no matter how powerful, even eagles must land to rest and eat. Remember, you can't fly forever. At some point, you need to stop and take care of your earthbound needs. Eagle energy encourages you to be courageous and to stretch your limits, to not accept the status quo, but to reach for the sky and become more than you believe you are capable of being.

Solar Plexus

The bald eagle is a very noble bird. It tends to soar through the air rather than flap its wings, holding them still and flat. In this chakra, the eagle says you do not need to prove anything to anyone. Whatever you undertake, you do so without questioning your ability. The eagle's place on the food chain is at the top, and this is likely a place you find yourself. Be it in your workplace or within a community, others recognize you as a natural leader. Another aspect of the eagle in this chakra comes from the spectacular aerial displays it performs to attract a mate or to protect its territory: a caution that it isn't necessary for you to take risks and show off. Your ability speaks for itself.

Heart

Both male and female eagles share in the building of the nest, gathering and arranging sticks as part of their bonding. This bonded pair will stay together for life; however, if one of them dies, most eagles will seek out another mate. For you, your partner must be an equal in all aspects of life, and the devotion between you must be sincere. If you are not in a partnership yet, don't settle for anyone but your match; you will only end up disappointed. If you have found your life partner, know that you are indeed blessed. If you are a widow or a widower, know that being with someone new does not dishonor the love you once shared. It is more likely that your late partner would want you to move on and find love again so that you aren't alone.

Throat

Though the eagle is large and powerful, its voice is very weak. Any sounds it makes are to communicate with its mate or to warn predators that an area is protected. As confident as you outwardly appear, you may have trouble speaking in front of other people. You might only be comfortable talking to people you know very well, particularly your mate. It could also be that you aren't one to speak very often, but when you do, it is with good reason and with a purpose in mind.

Third Eye

Eagles have very unusual eyes. Humans only have binocular vision, but eagles have both binocular and monocular vision, which means they can use their eyes together or independently, depending on what they are looking at. In addition, they have more light-sensitive cells than we do, giving them the ability to see color more vividly than humans, even perceiving different shades of the same color. Eagle eyesight is so keen the bird can spot even well-hidden prey from a very long distance. These abilities say that there is very little that escapes your awareness. You see things and pick up details that others miss. The eagle also gives you an advantage in the ethereal realms. If you are open to it and allow yourself, you can see beyond the three-dimensional world into the world of Spirit, and you might even see auras. If you are already aware of this ability, honor it.

Crown

In some cultures, the eagle was believed to be the first shaman, and in several religions, that eagle can touch the face of God. Eagle energy helps you see your life from a higher place than just your earthly one. Eagle is calling you to soar on its wings and reach the land of Spirit. In doing so, you will be able to not only gain a different perspective of your own life, but you will be able to see your interconnection to everything around you.

FOX

Researchers in Jordan opened a grave in a sixteen-thousand-year-old cemetery and found the remains of a man buried with his pet fox; the first-known human and pet dog buried together was not until about four thousand years later. While the fox is a member of the dog family (Canidae), it surprisingly has a lot in common with the cat: foxes have eyes with vertical slits, and the gray fox has semiretractable claws. They like to stalk and play with their food before eating it, and they can even climb trees.

Key Attributes

Seeing through deception, camouflage, cleverness, quick wit, alertness, agility, magic and cunning, femininity, gentleness, stealth, and keen insight.

Chakra Interpretations

Root

Foxes may return to their mates year after year, but they may also take on other partners as well. They don't live in packs but in a small family group with a dominant pair and several others, which may include maturing offspring or nonbreeding sisters that help with the rearing of the kits. During breeding season, a fox pair will work together to care for the cubs, and the male will support the female by bringing food for the family. Creating a warm and safe home is essential to you. You probably prefer a monogamous relationship, and you may even like living with extended family members. If you're female, you may rely a great deal on your female relations or sisters of choice when it comes to taking care of your family. If you are male, you may follow the old-fashioned, but still honorable, belief that it is your job to put food on the table but leave the care of the family to the females.

Sacral

Someone sexually attractive is often called *foxy*. You have no problem with sexual expression. Foxes are also known to be friendly and curious. They love to play and will often steal toys left out in a yard or golf balls from a golf course. Not only are they self-entertaining, but they love to play with other foxes and will also play with mammals such as cats and dogs. While you are perfectly happy entertaining yourself, other people think you are fun to be around, so don't always go it alone. Because the fox is nocturnal and usually only seen at dawn or dusk, this could be the time of day when you are at your most creative.

Solar Plexus

The fox has a legendary reputation for resourcefulness, earning it a reputation for intelligence and cunning. The fox will camouflage itself in its surroundings, and gray foxes can partially retract their claws, helping them climb trees to escape predators. This combination of skills allows you to view situations with detachment and clarity, and if you don't want people to see you, they won't. The fox is also capable of quick action, a warning to make sure you use your cunning and intelligence so your actions don't get you into trouble. Another trait of the fox is its uncanny sensitivity to its environment. If this applies to you, you can probably sense an incoming storm or any other shift in the weather. You may also be able to tell instantly if anything at all has changed or is "off" in your home or work environment.

Heart

As mentioned above, many foxes return to the same mate, but even those that do often sleep and hunt alone. You may be happiest when you are in a safe, monogamous relationship while maintaining your personal space. If you are married or cohabitating with a partner, you may even prefer sleeping in separate bedrooms. If you aren't married but are in a stable relationship, it might be that both of you prefer an arrangement of living in different places and only getting together for quality time. As far as friends go, you are very loyal, and your heart is playful, which means not only are you a good friend to have, but you collect good friends around you.

Throat

Foxes have incredibly sensitive hearing: they can hear a mouse squeak from as far away as a hundred feet. You too have sensitive hearing and can probably pick up details of sound that others miss. An example is listening to complex music and being able to sort out the different instruments or being able to hear conversations clearly even when in a crowd. Foxes also have a wide variety of vocalizations, and they love to communicate with each other through play. Most likely, you have a quick wit, so much so that some people have trouble keeping up with your conversational style. You might also be strong politically. You would be a persuasive council member or community representative, particularly if it involves the environment. You probably come out the winner in any verbal debate you are involved in. This is quite valuable if your career involves arguing law of any kind.

Third Eye

Fox eyes have vertical pupils like cat eyes, helping them see well in the dark. Because you can watch a situation without being observed, this speaks to your ability to see and hear what others miss. Some researchers believe that foxes can sense the earth's magnetic field and use it as a targeting system for pouncing on prey. The ability to sense these fields is called *magnetoreception*, and it is widespread in the animal kingdom. Though it is still being debated, some current research says humans also have this ability, though to a lesser degree and most aren't aware that they do. I personally believe that we do, and those of us who are sensitive often have an uncanny sense of direction.

Crown

As mentioned above, it is thought by some that foxes can sense the earth's magnetic fields and that they use this skill along with their remarkable hearing to catch prey. Open up to the perceptions of the fox and see what you can uncover about yourself and the world around you beyond your self-imposed limitations.

FROG

Frogs have an association with birth and rebirth that traces back to Egypt, Rome, and many other cultures from antiquity. Scientists call frogs an *indicator species* because they give insight to how an ecosystem is functioning. Frogs have very thin skin that they sometimes breathe through, so they easily absorb pollutants from their environment, which can harm or kill them. The presence of lots of frogs is a good indication that the ecosystem is healthy.

Key Attributes

Transition and transformation, emotional and physical healing, empathy, cleansing, renewal, rebirth, fertility, abundance, and ancient earth wisdom.

Chakra Interpretations

Root

Frogs live in a wide range of habitats, but most prefer areas that are damp. You probably prefer to live in a wet climate and don't do well in dry heat. While you might like to visit the ocean occasionally, your preference is wooded regions with streams, lakes, or ponds. In winter, you don't hibernate, but you do slow down, and once spring arrives, you can't wait to get out and soak up the sun. Spiritually, frogs represent emotional cleansing and healing. Call on frog energy if you want help clearing negativity and toxic energies from yourself or your surroundings.

Sacral

Frogs are social creatures, and a group of them is called an *army*. A group of male frogs will croak quite loudly to try to attract females. It is possible that when it comes to finding a life partner, you tend to be a bit verbose. You might even be part of a circle of very loud friends and think this is the way you will find love. Luckily for you, if this is the kind of circle you are happiest in and you don't already have a partner that is your equal, then this is exactly the kind of behavior that will attract one—your partner will be the same way.

Solar Plexus

One well-known fact about frogs is that they change, starting out life as tadpoles and transforming into frogs. What isn't as well-known is that this transformation continues throughout the frog's life. A frog completely sheds its skin on a regular basis and after it does, it eats the old skin. Boy, when you decide to transform yourself, you do it so thoroughly that you even devour who you used to be. Frog in this chakra could also mean that you have felt it is time for you to do this, to shed your old skin and become the person you want the world to see: your true self. If this doesn't ring true for you, note that most frogs can jump twenty times their body length. You are probably the kind of person who gets great satisfaction from jumping into action quickly, be it into a project, a task at work, or even a relationship.

Heart

Frogs absorb water into their body through their skin instead of drinking with their mouths. You tend to be very empathetic and use this skill as easily as most people breathe air. Your sensitivity can mean you sometimes unintentionally soak up other people's toxic energy. If this is the case, it is vital that you do personal cleansings on a regular basis. Frogs also have two natural survival skills: some have poisonous skin and some use camouflage. Are you hiding from the world or projecting toxic energy to protect yourself? Yet another aspect of the frog in this chakra speaks to the unfortunate fact that many of us, especially men, are taught not to cry. We learn to bottle up our feelings and block the emotional release we need. Working with frog energy will help your tears to flow like a cleansing rain.

Throat

In some traditions, the frog is a rainmaker that calls healing waters to the land. The croak of each species of frog is unique, and some frogs can be heard up to a mile away. You would do well using your voice for healing, especially when it comes to the environment. The influence of your voice could be felt even over long distances. A fun fact about frogs is that their ears are connected to their lungs. The eardrums, called *tympana*, are located behind their eyes, and the lungs equalize the pressure differences between the outer and inner surface of the eardrum, which allows the frog to be really loud without hurting its own ears. As mentioned, you might be part of a noisy group of friends, and you seem perfectly adapted for this kind of communication style.

Third Eye

The large protruding eyes that most frogs possess give them nearly 360-degree vision. Many frogs are nocturnal and have excellent night vision. In fact, recent studies have shown that they can see in full color even when it is so dark humans can't see anything at all. You very likely have excellent night vision or at the very least have sharp color perception. This is a helpful skill if you have to do a lot of driving at night or if you are an artist or decorator. The cleansing aspect of the frog may be an inspiration for you to transform your perspective, clearing away old beliefs that may be blocking you from truly *seeing*.

Crown

The transformative aspect of the frog may be saying that you are ready to, or are in the process of, transforming a spiritual practice. Is it time to shed old beliefs so you can be open to a new connection with your highest self or your definition of a higher power? Because of its association with water, frogs are spiritually linked to moon energy. If you are going through a transformation in your life, connect with how the frog sheds its skin and tie it to the phases of the moon. If you are looking for some sort of growth, start at the new moon, and if you are trying to change old habits, start at the full moon and visualize the shedding.

GROUSE

The grouse is a ground-dwelling bird that belongs to the subfamily of Tetraonidae and lives in temperate and subarctic regions of the Northern Hemisphere. The grouse can easily handle the cold northern winters because it has feathers in its nostrils and legs as well as feathers on its toes that act like snowshoes. During the winter, a grouse buries itself in the snow; this provides not only warmth but also protection from predators. The male grouse's signature drumming sound happens when the bird quickly rotates its wings forward and backward, forcing the air into a temporary vacuum, which generates a deep, thumping sound wave that carries up to a quarter of a mile. It's a remarkable sound to hear.

Key Attributes

The sacred spiral, drumming and dance, personal power, birth and rebirth, and life movement.

Chakra Interpretations

Root

Grouse live in forests, building a simple nest on the ground. Most likely, you like to live modestly, preferably near trees, and close to the earth, even if that means a ground-floor apartment or ranch-style house. You want to blend in with your surroundings, rather than attracting attention to yourself. Safety is probably your primary motivation, but it could also be shyness; either is fine as long as your home is what you want it to be. If you are an omnivore like the grouse, you probably aren't very picky about what you eat.

Sacral

When courting a female, the male grouse will puff up its chest and do a strutting dance to get attention. You may feel like you have to make yourself seem important in order to impress, including going overboard when you are trying to woo a potential mate because you are afraid the person you are pursuing won't like the real you, even if the person you are trying to woo is a potential employer. Try showing your true colors; you might be surprised that they will love you (or hire you) just the way you are. Another behavioral trait of grouse is that they will stand perfectly still if they feel threatened. If something in your life is causing you to feel scared stiff, it might be time for you to come out of your hiding place and fly away.

Solar Plexus

Because of their intricate coloring and patterns, grouse are so camouflaged that very often the only way to spot them is by listening for the rustling of dry leaves as they walk along the forest floor. Unlike most birds, whose colorings are nearly identical within a species, each individual grouse has a unique pattern on its tail feathers. It could be that you are shy, only making your presence known if you want it to be so. That said, while shy, you still like having something unique about your appearance that may not be obvious or visible to anyone other than the most observant. Maybe you have a tattoo (or a few) that you keep hidden. Maybe you have a single streak of bright color in your hair. Whatever it is, you do it for you because it is your identity and not out of a need for external expression. Another aspect of grouse in this chakra speaks to the fact that a young grouse is ready for independent life almost immediately after birth. Perhaps you left the nest at a very young age. If so, you have had an independent streak your entire life and are usually very sure of who you are and where you are going.

Heart

While many birds mate for life, the grouse stays solitary, and the male ruffed grouse stays aggressively territorial throughout his adult life. You may prefer being alone and may even get nasty if someone invades your privacy. However, the grouse is nature's drummer. Drums connect our hearts not only to the hearts of other drummers but also to the heartbeat of the earth. If the first interpretation of grouse in the heart chakra doesn't fit you, it could be that the grouse is calling you to find fellow drummers so you can experience that heartbeat.

Throat

The female grouse is generally quiet, and when it does make sound, it is usually a warning to her chicks. Most likely, you only like to speak when necessary, and when you do, you speak very softy. In the opposite of this, as mentioned earlier, the male ruffed grouse will puff up his chest to impress a female. This is a caution to make sure that when you do speak, you aren't just full of hot air. What is important is to speak with authenticity.

Third Eye

While ruffed grouse have excellent eyesight, sage grouse do not. In fact, because of poor vision, they have been known to fly into barbed wire fences and even wind turbines. It might be that you need to watch where you are going because you tend to act without forethought, and that often lands you in trouble. From a spiritual perspective, it could be that you fly headlong into a new psychic exploration without taking the time to find out if it is a good fit for you. Another possibility is that your psychic side has blinders on. If this is the case and you want to open that door, just drop them and allow that vision to improve.

Crown

The grouse, being a ground-dwelling bird, is an excellent ally to call on if you have trouble being grounded while you are meditating. Connecting with grouse energy may help open you to the earth's energies and possibly even the cosmic ones. Grouse energy is also very connected to movement and the spiral dance. Get outside, go barefoot, stomp your feet, join a drum circle, or try a spiral dance ceremony so you can feel the heartbeat of the earth and connect with other people.

HAWK

Currently, there are over two hundred species of hawks around the world, approximately twenty-five of which are in North America. These highly intelligent birds live in a variety of habitats including marshes, forests, rainforests, prairies, open savannas, grasslands, mountains, and coastal regions. Some evidence suggests that hawks were used in the art of falconry as early as 2000 BCE. Falconry was considered a status symbol and favorite sport amongst the nobles of medieval Europe, the ancient Middle East, and the Mongolian Empire. Ancient Celts believed that the hawk was a messenger from the Otherworld. In some Native American tribes, hawks represent protection from enemies. In Polynesian legends, hawks are birds of prophecy with healing powers. For the most part, I reference the red-tailed hawk in the interpretations below because it is the most common in North America.

Key Attributes

Power of vision, intuition, observation, intelligence, wisdom, courage, dignity, truth, recalling past lives, guardianship, authority, leadership, messages from Spirit, understanding the original mission of your soul, and achieving one's goals through perseverance.

Chakra Interpretations

Root

Red-tailed hawks can adapt to life pretty much anywhere there is open habitat, and they build their nests in the tops of tall trees and even on cliffs and building ledges. Most likely, you can adapt to life anywhere—what matters is that you have an unobstructed view—and you are probably very territorial about your home or personal space. In addition, hawks are carnivores. If you can relate to this aspect of a hawk, it could be that you love to eat meat. Their exceptional eyesight helps them spot prey from very high in the sky, and they will chase it tirelessly until they catch it. This aspect speaks to your being willing to go the distance when it comes to survival. You will work long hours or even multiple jobs so you can pay your bills and put food on the table.

Sacral

In a similar vein as the message above, a hawk will fly tirelessly to catch what it wants. Like the hawk, you work hard to pursue your passions and can overcome any obstacle in your path. You might even be the kind of person who will go long hours without sleep and may even forget to eat or take care of your personal needs because you are so focused on your goal. That is an honorable trait but try to remember to rest now and then; it might even give you a fresh perspective. As with most birds of prey, the female hawk is larger than the male. If you are in a relationship, whichever one of you identifies as more feminine is probably taller or larger than the masculine member of your partnership.

Solar Plexus

Hawks are very powerful, confident birds. You project a strong sense of self to the world; combine that with your intense focus, and very little ruffles your feathers. Your observational skills give you steely instincts, which may mean that your first impressions are rarely wrong. In addition, you exude an invisible power that everyone you meet can sense. You have a strong sense of optimism that is contagious to those around you. Other people seem to want to stand taller and straighter when you are around.

Heart

Red-tailed hawks are monogamous, most mating for life. The male hawk performs a spectacular aerial dance to attract a mate. If you are like the red-tailed hawk, you are probably quite romantic and like to show off to a potential partner, and once you catch the right one, you will stay together for life. If you connect more with other hawks, such as the Cooper's hawk, you may be romantic and monogamous while you are in a relationship but don't necessarily stay with the same person for life. You might be happiest this way, or it could just be you haven't found your match yet.

Throat

The hawk's confidence means that it has no issues or fear when it comes to using its voice. Most likely, you are not one that suffers from stage fright; quite the opposite is probably true. When it is your time to speak, be it on stage, in a business meeting, or just in casual conversation, you do so with clarity, purpose, and confidence. The hawk shows you can lead and influence others with your voice and could be telling you it's time to take the initiative and commit to a more active role.

Third Eye

There is good reason for the saying someone is *hawkeyed*: hawks notice everything. They have excellent eyesight and can see as much as eight times better than humans. They can see not only the visible range but also the ultraviolet part of the spectrum. Hawk vision will not only give you the ability to see from a higher perspective, but it will also help you spot details and interpret signs that others miss. It is very likely that you have or can develop the ability to see into the spirit realm or see ley lines.

Crown

One of the hawk's totem meanings is a messenger from the spirit realm. You already have a direct connection to your higher power and can communicate with it with confidence and ease. Hawk in this chakra can also be saying that you are awakening to your soul's purpose—your reason for this incarnation. One suggestion is to do meditations that tap into your Akashic records. Since the hawk spends a great deal of its time aloft, this means that even when you soar, you stay grounded in reality.

HERON

Whether standing patiently at the edge of a pond or flying, the great blue heron is a majestic sight to behold. While flying, this bird curls its neck into an S shape, stretches its long legs out behind it in a straight line, and gracefully glides on a wingspan that can reach over six feet. Currently, there are more than sixty different species of herons, varying in size and color and inhabiting wetlands around the world. The great blue heron is the most common one in North America and is the one I use for the interpretations listed below. It is also one of the symbols for the Chesapeake Bay Trust. I spent the first fifteen years of my life near one of the rivers off the bay, so it is a place near and dear to my heart.

Key Attributes

Self-reliance and confidence, self-reflection, independence, grace, resourcefulness, introspection, being present, intuition, taking personal responsibility and accountability, achieving one's goals through patience and planning.

Chakra Interpretations

Root

One potential aspect of the heron says that while individually solitary, herons tend to nest in large colonies. They usually build their nests high up in trees away from potential ground predators. You might feel most at home living in a high-rise apartment setting, especially if it has a water view. You may not ever know your neighbors but still feel like there is safety in numbers. Another possibility says that while herons are carnivores and will eat anything they can grab, their preference seems to be for seafood. This could be saying that while you don't have an aversion to eating meat, you prefer fish or shellfish in your regular diet.

Herons are most active during dusk and dawn because those are the best times for fishing, as any angler will attest. Most likely, these are the times during the day that you feel the most alive and alert.

Sacral

Herons are what is called *seasonally monogamous*, meaning they are only with one partner at a time and only for a short time; they do not find a life match. Like the heron, when you are in a relationship, it tends to be monogamous, but you are perfectly happy being alone. You aren't someone who requires a lot of people in your life. Another behavioral trait of the heron is that it hunts by waiting patiently for its prey and then quickly striking to catch it. When it comes to pursuing your passions, nothing and no one can rush you. You do everything at your own pace. You focus your attention, letting nothing distract you, and wait until the timing is perfect before you take any decisive action. From a more humorous perspective, the heron in this chakra could mean that one of your life's passions is fishing!

Solar Plexus

Herons are very striking birds. It could be that your physical structure is tall and slender, but even if it isn't, you exude silent elegance like the heron. You are perfectly comfortable on your own, following your own instincts and guidance and your own path of self-determination. You have no desire or need to keep up with the material world. You stand out in a crowd because of your uniqueness. Other people may be mystified by your aloofness, so if this bothers someone you care about, it may be necessary to explain that your behavior isn't meant to hurt them; it is just who you are. Another possible connection speaks to the heron's patience. Because you are one to watch a situation carefully, your gut instincts are usually spot-on.

Heart

The heron acknowledges that solitude can be a healthy practice, that it's okay to be alone. While usually solitary, both male and female herons will work together to make a nest. The heron's lesson is that even the most independent among us admit that there are some areas of life where a partnership makes life a little easier and can work if both parties reach an agreement and respect each other's need for independence.

Throat

One aspect of heron for you could be that words sometimes get stuck in your throat, especially if you tend to talk so fast that your thoughts get ahead of you. Heron energy can teach you the wisdom of waiting patiently before speaking. Slow down, take a deep breath, and refuse to be rushed no matter how much pressure you feel. Let the heron's S-curved neck slow down your words so that when you do speak, it is with dignity and forethought.

Third Eye

Due to the number of the photoreceptors within a heron's eyes, they can see more detail than we can and can also see at night. In addition to having patience, not only can you see the metaphorical forest *and* the tress, but you can probably see the veins in the leaves as well. This just means that nothing escapes your understanding. Most likely, your psychic perception and insight are equally sharp. If your busy life is getting in the way of you being open to your intuition, heron energy can teach you how to slow down and learn patience so you can hear what your hunches are trying to tell you.

Crown

The heron has inherent stability, balance, and grace. These elements, along with patience, show that you already do or can learn how to open your spiritual awareness through stillness. You might want to try standing meditations such as those found in qigong and yoga. Finding serenity will help you be open to any messages from the spirit realms that are trying to fly in.

HORSE

Considered by many to be the noblest of all creatures, the horse evolved from a much smaller animal. It is believed horses first became domesticated in Asia about five thousand years ago, and they have been our companions ever since. In heavily wooded states like Vermont, draft horses are used to stretch cable for high-tech communication systems because they can maneuver through areas with no road access with little to no damage to the ecosystem. Therapeutic riding is used to help children and adults with special needs as wide-ranging as physical limitations, developmental issues, and PTSD. A fun fact is that while the state of Maryland (my home state) doesn't have an individual state animal, the official state sport is jousting!

Key Attributes

Unconditional love, empathy, loyalty, freedom, mobility, collaboration with and serving others, awakening inner power, dignity, and new journeys.

Chakra Interpretations

Root

There is a lot of debate over if horses should wear shoes or not, but many agree that it comes down to what the horse does on a regular basis (e.g., if it's a working horse, pulling heavy weight) and what the terrain is like where it lives (e.g., if it needs shoes to protect it from wet conditions or rocks). In an ideal world, barefoot is better. You probably love to go barefoot (or sock footed) in your home, but most of us can't do that at our jobs. It is important for you to have the correct foundation footwear as it relates to what you do for your living or what your activities involve. For some this means steel-toed boots, for others it might mean slip-resistant shoes, and some may be able to just wear what they like. What is important is to be sure that what is on your feet makes you feel grounded and gives you a firm foundation.

Sacral

There has always been a connection between young girls coming into sexual maturity and horses. Then there are the stories of virgins and unicorns. *Stallion* is a term used not only for horses but also a sexually attractive man. The horse symbolizes power and can symbolize sexual power. You are probably very comfortable with your sexuality and your ability to express it. You enjoy riding on a wave of passion. If it isn't physical sex that is your passion, most likely creative expression is. Everything you do and all the ways you express yourself are full of intensity—you don't do anything halfway.

Solar Plexus

The horse is a powerful creature whose energy says you are in touch with your body's natural rhythm, self-worth, and personal power. We have all heard the expression "If you fall off a horse, the best thing you can do is get right back on." No matter what knocks you down, you just get back up and start again. If an obstacle is in your way, you find a way around or over it. Another lesson from the horse is to make sure to pace yourself. While horses can run within hours after being born, you may not want to charge right out of the gate without knowing what the ground underneath you is like or if you could be running full speed directly into a wall.

Heart

Horses have incredible intelligence. They understand our words, and their memory is equal to that of elephants. Like many other animals, they grieve the passing or loss of a companion. If you treat a horse kindly, it will remember you for as long as it lives and will instantly resume your friendship if it sees you again, regardless of how long you have been apart. Horses are also very social and will get lonely if left alone; they need to be part of a community. They tend to be empathetic and can be remarkably gentle. When you make a real friend, you will keep that friend for life, even if many years pass between times you see each other. In addition, you will go out of your way to help others, be it helping them move, lifting their spirits, or just being present with them in times of emotional need.

Throat

Horses express their moods and feelings through facial expressions using their ears, eyes, and nostrils. Horses also have a broad range of different vocalizations that vary depending on the situation. Most likely, people can read you like a book based on your facial expressions, and you can read theirs. You are also perfectly willing to speak your mind and will change your voice and tone depending on the situation or with whom you are talking. Miscommunication is a rare thing with you.

Third Eye

A horse's eyes are larger than the eyes of any other mammal that lives on land. They have three eyelids—two ordinary ones and a third called the *nictitating membrane* that occasionally sweeps the eye, lubricating and cleaning it. A horse's lower retina sees objects at a distance, and the upper retina is for closer viewing. Because their eyes are on the side of their head, not forward facing like ours, they can see nearly 360 degrees, but they have blind spots directly in front and behind them. You see both the distant future and the current situation but sometimes might miss what is right in front of you. It is also possible that you are easily startled if someone sneaks up behind you. Just try not to kick them if they do.

Crown

Horses are able to doze while standing up, but if they want to reach REM sleep, they need to lie down. Luckily, they don't need a lot of deep sleep. You could be the kind of person who gets by on very little sleep, and when you do sleep it is very deep and your dreams are likely vivid. If you are having trouble getting grounded, as mentioned earlier for the heron, you may want to consider standing forms of meditation. Horses have been known to show up in dreams as spirit guides, so if one appears to you, it is an invitation to ride on its back into the spiritual realms.

HUMMINGBIRD

The hummingbird is the smallest member of the bird family and is nicknamed simply *hummer* due to the sound its wings make when it flies. Hummingbirds can only be found in the Western Hemisphere, and of the more than three hundred known species, only twelve spend the summer in North America. Some hummers are so small that they can be caught in a spiderweb. Hummingbirds cannot walk or hop, but they can scoot sideways while perched. Their wings move imperceptibly fast, yet they can come to a complete stop after traveling at full speed and are the only birds that can fly backward. They have incredible endurance, migrate long distances, and return to the same gardens every year. Hummingbirds can remember every flower they have been to and how long it will take that flower to refill. Anyone who has ever kept hummingbird feeders knows that the birds will alert the household humans when their feeder is empty by hovering close by or even in front of a window to get their attention.

Key Attributes

Love, adaptability, resilience, joy, playfulness, ability to travel great distances, and tasting the sweetness of life.

Chakra Interpretations

Root

Hummingbirds are very territorial and, despite their tiny size, will aggressively chase away other hummingbirds and other types of birds. You probably have territorial instincts as well. It is difficult to care for hummingbirds in captivity because they are very fragile, and unless they are allowed to fly freely in a large area, they will likely die. The hummer shows that for your survival, you cannot be tied down or confined. You must have free movement but also need to return to familiar places. It could be that your preference is for a house with an open concept design and not a traditional home with divided rooms. Another aspect of the hummer is that they use their feet only for perching. You might have a tendency to stay in motion most of the time and have a hard time relaxing or getting grounded.

Sacral

Like many larger birds, a male hummingbird will perform a dramatic aerial display, moving his wings even faster than usual and flying in an arc to catch a female's attention. Once he mates with her, he moves on to the next pretty thing that catches his eye. As far as sex is concerned, while it may seem unflattering, you might love the theatrics of catching the attention of someone you have your eye on. Once you do, it is likely that you bore quickly and move on to the next conquest. For you, it could be about the game and not so much about finding someone with whom you can have an emotional connection. A more traditional aspect of hummer speaks to adaptability and resiliency while keeping a playful and optimistic outlook. The hummingbird could be a reminder to lighten up and stop taking life so seriously.

Solar Plexus

Hummingbirds are the tiniest of all birds but can be surprisingly aggressive. Because of your outward appearance, people may have a misguided opinion of your abilities or temper. Both may come as quite a shock once they get to know you. In addition to being the tiniest, hummers are also one of the brightest and most colorful types of birds, but they can hide or highlight those bright colors depending on where they face in relation to sunlight. One possible meaning for the hummingbird in this chakra is that there are times you prefer to hide in the shadows and times you like to shine in the spotlight. Try not to be afraid to show your truest, most beautiful self and shine more!

Heart

A hummingbird's breathing and heartbeat are so fast they use up a tremendous amount of energy. From a health standpoint, it could be that you suffer from high blood pressure or you occasionally are out of breath. If this is the case, taking care of your health is essential. Slowing down and adding meditative breathing exercises could be a great benefit. If your heart has suffered damage, working with hummingbird energy may be able to help you develop a lightness of being so you can heal enough to reopen to the people who care for you. From a domestic perspective, all hummingbird moms are single moms, so this could symbolize that you are a single parent.

Throat

Hummingbirds have a bill designed explicitly for sipping nectar from tubular flowers. Most likely, you have a bit of a sweet tooth! You probably have a unique way of communicating and tend to sugarcoat your words to keep from hurting someone. If this is the case, just make sure you are maintaining authenticity, or your words will sour over time. Another possibility is very simply that you enjoy tasting all the sweetness that life has to offer.

Third Eye

Hummingbirds can see color as well as humans, and they can also see in the ultraviolet spectrum. Because they fly so fast and can change direction quickly, they need excellent eyesight to keep them from flying into things. If you have experience with or include trance work in your practice, the hummingbird in this chakra could be saying that you are not the kind of person who needs or wants a long lead-in or guidance to enter a trance. Most likely, by the time you close your eyes, you are where you want to be. Another aspect speaks to the hummingbird's connection to nature spirits, especially those allied to flowers: you see the beauty in all things.

Crown

The hummer's iridescent wings move in a figure eight pattern, the symbol for infinity and a lesson for you to go beyond time, to stop moving so fast and learn to hover in the moment. Only then can you genuinely touch what is sacred and see what is beautiful. The hummer's iridescence is a reminder to reflect on the magic all around you, even in the smallest of things.

LIZARD

Lizards have been on earth for more than two hundred million years. They are cold-blooded and tend to be active during the day because they rely on the sun for warmth. Some lizard species have developed a defense mechanism called *autotomy*, in which they can drop their tail if they feel threatened. One fun thing about lizards is that they are born with a natural third eye at the top of their heads called a *parietal eye*, which senses light.

Key Attributes

Conservation of energy, paying attention to one's dreams, intuition, ability to cut your losses and leave the past behind, and psychic perception.

Chakra Interpretations

Root

Lizards are solitary creatures and do not require the company of others, except for the desert night lizard, which lives in a family group. Most likely, you are pretty private and rarely feel the need to socialize. When you do, it is with just a few people or family members. There is a part of the human brain responsible for our most primal survival instincts, our fight-or-flight reactions, often called our *lizard brain*. If you are dealing with a hazardous situation or a great deal of stress, it may be time to take a break or reach out for help, instead of fighting as a first reaction. Or, as mentioned above, some lizards can separate their tails, so it may be time to cut your losses and run.

Sacral

Nearly all lizards are solitary creatures that only come together to reproduce. For reproduction to occur, as with most living beings on the planet, most lizards still require a male and a female. However, there are a few species of lizard capable of asexual reproduction. It could be that sex doesn't matter to you very much, but you would like to have a child. If you are a woman and you don't want to be in a permanent relationship, modern science may be able to help you conceive through in vitro fertilization. If you are a man, you may be able to have a child the same way; you just need to find a woman willing to carry your child to term. Another aspect of the lizard, not related to sex but still related to pleasure, says you might love and need to spend time in the sun. If you suffer from seasonal depression due to lack of sunlight, get yourself a full spectrum lamp and spend time near it during the day.

Solar Plexus

Chameleons can change color, and they do this not only as a form of communication but also for camouflage. It may be that you feel like you need to change so you fit in or so you can hide. It could also be that you haven't yet decided who you are or who you want to be. This aspect of lizard will help you as you try on different identities until you find the one that fits for you. Just make sure it is who *you* want to be and not the identity someone else is demanding you assume. As mentioned above, some lizards can detach their tails if a predator catches them. Lizard energy could be asking you if it is time to walk away from old patterns, habits, or self-images that are threatening your ability to follow your dreams.

Heart

Most lizards are solitary creatures. However, one species, the shingleback skink, is thought to stay with the same partner long-term. Most likely, you are perfectly fine being a solitary person, but try to remember not to pass up a potential opportunity if you do find that rare partner. Your partner may be equally introverted, and the two of you may be able to find a beautiful balance between solitude and partnership. Another aspect in this chakra is a reminder that even if you have endured a great deal of tragedy and your heart has suffered as a result, the power of regeneration and renewal is within you.

Throat

Like a snake, a lizard sticks out its tongue to smell the air. You prefer to take in information about a situation before you speak. The chameleon aspect of the lizard could be asking if you have a habit of changing what you want to say to be safe or to feel like you fit in. Remember that sometimes it is okay to stand out and speak your truth. Male lizards perform a push-up or head-bobbing action as a form of communication with other males. Whereas many species use sound or bodily fluids to claim their territory, it is thought this action serves the same purpose. It is also a display of prowess and strength, much like showing off at the gym. The lizard in this chakra could mean that you aren't comfortable speaking; you prefer to let your actions speak for themselves.

Third Eye

As mentioned earlier, many lizards have a third eye on the top of their heads. This third eye doesn't see images but is sensitive to light and dark. It is possible that you were born with this chakra open. If this is the case, hopefully you had support as a child to understand what was happening to you. If not and you were taught or forced to ignore it, know that you can reopen this eye at any time. You were gifted with this for a reason, and it isn't something to fear. Finally, chameleons can move their eyes independently, which means they can look in two different directions at the same time. Not only are you able to see the world in a spectrum different from most people, but you can see multiple situations simultaneously.

Crown

In some traditions, the lizard is a symbol of the dreamer and visionary. When we dream, our minds download information and perceptions that we may not be conscious of in our waking life in symbolic ways. If you have trouble remembering your dreams, one way to get better at it is to keep a dream journal or just a notepad next to your bed. When you wake up, write down the first few words that pop into your head so that later when you have time for quiet meditation, those trigger words can help you with recall.

MOOSE

Moose can be found living in the northern United States, Canada, and Europe—anywhere that has seasonal snow cover—and they are the official state animal of Maine. The moose is the largest member of the deer family and, depending on the species, can weigh up to sixteen hundred pounds and stand over six feet tall at the shoulders. Add to that a considerable head and rack of antlers, and you have an enormous and majestic beast. Despite their size, moose can run fast: they can trot at a steady 20 miles per hour and for short distances can run up to 35 miles an hour. Moose calves grow quickly and can outrun a human at just five days old. They are born swimmers and can paddle over ten miles in one trip. They can close their nostrils underwater, which allows them to submerge completely so they can dive down to nibble underwater grasses.

Key Attributes

Self-esteem; courage; the joy of accomplishment; being full of contradictions, including being clumsy but graceful, fast but silent; wisdom; psychic awakening; and achieving goals by being headstrong.

Chakra Interpretations

Root

Moose are herbivores, so the moose's presence in the root chakra could be that you are a vegetarian. Moose also tend to be solitary creatures, except for a one-to-two-year period in which the mother will stay with her young. Although not proven through academic observation, some people who live where moose are prevalent and love watching their behavior believe that a male calf may be chased off once he becomes an adult, but female calves occasionally stay with their mom for several years. If you identify with a more masculine tendency, maybe you moved out at a very young age to make it on your own. If you lean more toward feminine tendencies, maybe you preferred to stay home and close to the person you identify as a mother figure. Interestingly, if a mother moose is healthy, it is not uncommon for her to have two calves instead of just one. It could be that you are a twin or that you have children that are twins.

Sacral

Moose are active throughout the day but are most active during sunrise and sunset. If you work all day, you're probably energetic early in the morning and get a second wind as the sun goes down. Another aspect of the moose in your sacral chakra relates to how much moose love to swim. Swimming helps moose regulate their body temperature and takes the stress off their bones and joints. If you aren't already an avid swimmer, you might want to start swimming on a regular basis. It will be beneficial for your health and might develop into a new passion.

Solar Plexus

Though very large, a moose can camouflage itself. You are one that can easily stand out in a crowd, but you are equally able to disappear if the situation calls for it. Perhaps you have always been taller or have a more substantial presence than your peers, and this makes them feel intimidated by you. If you want people to feel this way about you, you can do it with ease; however, if you want people to know a gentler you, you may have to work at it consciously.

Heart

The moose is antisocial, except for mating. You probably spend most of your time alone, rarely seeking out companionship, and when you do, it is only for physical release. You're fine with that, but just make sure your partner is too. On a different note, a mother moose is very protective and will deliver a powerful kick to fight off predators in defense of her young. It could be that you are very protective of anyone that you feel is under your care, and you have no qualms about wounding anyone or anything that tries to harm them. In addition, the moose has very poor eyesight. The moose could be asking if you are missing an opportunity for love because you are blind to someone that is already in your life.

Throat

Moose make a variety of vocalizations, some of which can be heard from miles away. Once a male moose answers the call of a female, he will race to be with her and will run down or fight anything or anyone that gets in his way. Most likely, you are very headstrong, and if you are on a mission or have a goal in mind, there is nothing and no one that can stop you. This is an admirable quality to have, but it's also a reminder to be aware of whom you are stepping on or hurting in the process. Another aspect of the moose in this chakra could be that when your mate or partner calls, you will drop everything and run to their side. An interesting fact is that moose can move each ear independently; this symbolizes that you want to hear multiple sides of a story before you jump to any conclusions.

Third Eye

Male moose are very territorial, and you never want to look them in the eye because they view direct eye contact as a sign of aggression. It is possible that you have trouble looking people in the eye, that you tend to see it as a challenge. Try to remember that not everyone is out to get you or invade your territory. Moose babies are born with their eyes open, which could signify that you have been *aware* your entire life. If you want to, you can tap into the innocent psychic vision you had as a child. As mentioned, moose can move each ear independently, but, odd in the animal world, they can move their eyes independently too. This is a further indication that you may have had this chakra open most of your life and can see both the physical and metaphysical worlds simultaneously.

Crown

A moose's antlers weigh around forty pounds. If you are carrying the weight of the world on your shoulders, it may be keeping you from opening to your higher self. Another way to look at the moose in this chakra is to turn those antlers into a natural satellite dish and tune into any frequency you want—especially the natural world.

MOUNTAIN LION

The mountain lion sits at the top of the food chain and helps balance local wildlife populations. They are solitary creatures and very territorial. Considered opportunistic ambush hunters, they are nocturnal and hunt alone between dusk and dawn. A fun fact about these cats is that they hold the Guinness record (at least as of this writing) for the animal with the most names: over forty in English alone, and more than two hundred in total, including puma, mountain lion, catamount, panther, and ghost cat.

Key Attributes

Courage, power, strength, silence, dignity, nobility, guardianship, patience, self-assurance, intuition, ability to take charge of a situation, primal feminine grace, sensuality, and the capacity to claim one's power or authority.

Chakra Interpretations

Root

As mentioned above, mountain lions are very territorial and require a lot of room. In fact, only a few cats can survive within a thirty-square-mile area, and only by a system of mutual avoidance. You have a stubborn nature and need a great deal of personal space and solitude. Even if you are in a relationship, you need a lot of alone time. Others may not understand that, but as long as you make it clear to anyone you care about that it isn't about them, they will learn to respect this need without being hurt. Another aspect of the mountain lion in this chakra speaks to the fact that the mountain lions will travel long distances in search of food. You could have a long commute for your job and are always relieved to finally get home.

Sacral

All cats have a natural sensuality, and the mountain lion acknowledges that you are comfortable in your skin and have an innate, voluptuous mystique. Mountain lions are solitary, so perhaps your perfect match is someone else with mountain lion energy. As far as creative passions are concerned, whatever you undertake, you do so with clarity and confidence, never wavering from or questioning your talent or skill. You may be someone who likes to hide out in your studio and do nothing but create, be it writing, art, or music. Those are the passions that drive you and help you feel alive.

Solar Plexus

You carry yourself with confidence while still respecting the personal space of others. Being a leader comes naturally to you, and you are someone who can lead from a position of strength and intelligence and not from the need to control. Your very presence exudes leadership and few people challenge or question your right to the role. This elusive cat can also be a caution not to be too independent and lose connection to others and the world around you. Another trait of the animal is patience. A mountain lion will hide silently before pouncing on its prey, waiting for the perfect moment to act. This says you are someone who does their due diligence and research before committing to anything. You take your time to observe and won't act until you know the timing is right. You have learned through experience that doing so ensures your success.

Heart

As confident as the mountain lion seems, it is afraid of humans and will try to avoid them. Most likely, you are very self-assured but may be fearful of opening your heart to another. The only time a mountain lion lives with others is when the mother is raising her kittens; the father is never present. It could be that you are a single parent and your children mean everything to you. The definition for *children* isn't necessarily human; it could be companion animals or even plants. The key interpretation here is that you tend to give your heart not to a partner but to those who cannot care for themselves. Another possibility is if you are in a relationship, it is most likely with someone who has an equally strong independent streak, and you respect each other's need for autonomy.

Throat

As with many predator species, communication is typically achieved through scent marking one's territory. It is possible that you like to wear some form of fragrance, and your scent tends to linger after you have left the room, letting people know that you have been there. Little is known about vocalization in the wild because most of the studies have been done with cats that are in captivity, but it has been observed that the mother communicates with her kittens in a variety of ways. It may be that you aren't comfortable talking with other adults, that you may prefer talking to children or your pets. You may even be a grade school teacher. A word of caution that relates back to patience: while you are usually very tolerant, it is possible for you to lash out quickly with little or no warning if annoyed or threatened. If this is the case for you, it may be wise to learn how to take a breath so you are sure the recipient is deserving of your wrath.

Third Eye

Mountain lions have excellent night vision, and their field of vision is much greater than ours. All of this could be saying that you see the big picture in all situations. As mentioned above, these cats have incredible patience and will stare at an object or potential prey, unmoving, for what may seem like an eternity. This says that you have intense focus, clarity of vision, and perseverance.

Crown

The mountain lion in this chakra says that when you connect with Spirit, you do so from a position of equality, pride, and respect, not from a fearful posture or one of ego. Most likely, your spiritual practice is solitary—just you and what you identify as a higher power—and you don't feel the need to practice with other people. Possibly, you use your leadership skills to guide others in ways to connect with their higher selves so they can do so without fear.

MOUSE

The mouse is a very hardy creature, capable of living in a wide variety of terrains, and comes in a wide range of colors and sizes. Currently, there are close to forty known species of mice. Mice typically make burrows underground if they live out in the wild, but as everyone knows, they are perfectly happy in human attics and walls. Because they are nocturnal, we typically only hear them at night. Though stereotypically considered messy, mice are very clean and tidy, and just like humans, their homes are broken out into different rooms, including a bedroom for sleeping, a "kitchen" for storing food, and even a bathroom for doing their business. The mouse has fantastic balance and can walk along narrow pieces of rope or wire, scale rough vertical surfaces, and can slip through spaces as small as a dime.

Key Attributes

Paying attention to details, industriousness, heightened awareness, determination, cleverness, shyness, and nitpicky organization to the point of obsession.

Chakra Interpretations

Root

A mouse is very territorial. Even a domestic mouse likes to have a place it can call its own. A female mouse will make a nest out of anything she can find, including chewed-up wires, books, papers, and insulation. Like the mouse, you are very resourceful. You can create a safe and comfortable home pretty much anywhere and with anything. You might even be the king or queen of DIY projects—taking someone else's trash and turning it into treasure. You probably do your best work at night, making sounds that keep the neighbors guessing.

Sacral

A mouse uses facial expressions to communicate their mood to others. Most likely, your friends and family can read your facial expressions like a book. You are no good at hiding your feelings. If you are tense about something, you might come across as scattered and a little hyper. You probably also have an inquisitive nature. You love to explore places you've never been and try things you've never tried. You love to try new creative things and get easily sparked by new ideas, but this may leave you with a workshop or studio filled with unfinished projects. Another passion you may have is food. Mice will eat fifteen to twenty times a day. You probably love food and tend to nibble throughout the day, but there is a good chance your body doesn't show it because your metabolism runs high.

Solar Plexus

Not surprisingly, most wild mice are afraid of humans and other animals, but they are very social with each other. Domestic mice are very friendly toward humans they know and trust and make excellent pets for older children and adults. Have you lost your confidence, or have you been timid your whole life? You probably feel comfortable around an intimate group of close friends or family, but being out in the world terrifies you. You tend to scurry for the nearest hiding place when faced with anything new. Take a breath and try finding the stillness within. Look at the situation from a safe distance to see if you genuinely need to hide or if it's force of habit.

Heart

A mouse's heart can beat anywhere from just over three hundred to more than eight hundred beats per minute. This could mean that you are prone to high blood pressure or possibly have a fearful, racing heart. If this is the case, make sure you regularly visit a doctor to keep on top of it. Adding a meditation practice may help you learn calm. Just like many inherited diseases are passed on through our blood, a mouse passes its fear instinct on to its babies and grandbabies through its DNA. It is possible that you are carrying generational habits and anxieties that you picked up not by your own life experience but by the experiences of your ancestors. This is hard to determine if you don't know your family's history or stories. If you think this might be the case, try doing some ancestor work to heal those past traumas so you can release them. Your ancestors will thank you.

Throat

The mouse is an intelligent creature with sophisticated levels of communication, using sounds both audible and ultrasonic, beyond the range of human hearing. For you, the cliché "quiet as a mouse" could mean that you have a lot of trouble expressing yourself in any way. You know you're smart and have a lot of creative thoughts and ideas, but you may be afraid to show them for fear of being gobbled up or attacked. It may be time for your inner mouse to become a lion and learn how to roar.

Third Eye

Mice have poor eyesight but make up for this with their exceptional hearing and smell. A mouse can also feel temperature changes through their whiskers. You have the natural-born gift of intense awareness of your surroundings. You can sense danger long before anyone else, and you may have a sensitivity to place memory. If you are feeling uneasy about something and there is no logical reason why, try removing yourself from wherever you are and see if the feeling passes. If this takes place in your home, try smudging to cleanse the area of residual emotions.

Crown

A mouse's inherited fear could signify that connecting with your definition of a higher power terrifies you. It could be that as a young child you were taught that the unknown was evil or something to fear. You may feel like you are too small and can't possibly connect with something so big and unknowable. Just remember another famous line—"all creatures great and small"—and know that while you may think you are insignificant, you are loved by Spirit, and it wants you to connect. Be brave—the universe isn't going to eat you!

OCTOPUS

In the class Cephalopoda, there are approximately three hundred currently known species of octopus to be found in the earth's oceans. Most cultures view these mysterious mollusks with a sense of awe, wonder, and often fear, and they have been the inspiration for legends like the kraken of Norway and the lusca of the Caribbean. The octopus has three hearts, blue blood, and a central brain, though most of its neurons are found in its arms. This means each arm can taste, touch, and move autonomously after receiving the initial command from the brain.

Key Attributes

Adaptability, resourcefulness, achieving goals with flexibility, high intelligence, grace, camouflage, and strong defenses.

Chakra Interpretations

Root

The octopus can only live in salt water. This means you probably love being near the ocean; the smell of the sea is life to you. Another connection you may have could be to the octopus's diet, the majority of which is shellfish. While the octopus has a cartilaginous "skull," it has no skeletal structure, which allows it to contort itself so that it can squeeze through spaces much smaller than its body. Octopuses typically will create a den to live in for a few weeks but will even crawl into a bottle or some other trash that has found its way to the bottom of the sea floor. Most likely, you move around a lot, so you keep very few personal possessions. It could be that your job demands this, or it could be personal preference. It is very possible that you are called to tiny-house or RV living; key for you is to be able to move on whenever the spirit moves you.

Sacral

The octopus doesn't do well in captivity. It is important to your emotional sanity that you don't feel caged in. If someone or something tries to contain you, you will do everything in your power to gain your freedom. Also, an octopus is driven by intelligence rather than instinct. As mentioned earlier, they don't just have one brain like humans do but rather have one central brain, and each arm is capable of acting independently. You are the kind of person who doesn't let your passions rule your life; you think about everything. At the same time, you probably have a lot of projects going on simultaneously, and you give each one equal attention.

Solar Plexus

The octopus is known for being able to change its color to blend in with its surroundings, and one species, the mimic octopus, can even change its appearance and behavior to impersonate other sea creatures. The octopus in this chakra means you intentionally blend in wherever you are. This could be because you don't want to stand out, but it could also be for safety reasons. The octopus's movement is also key for this chakra. They can leisurely float along the ocean floor, swim very fast, or shoot off in a sudden burst of speed when threatened, usually leaving behind a cloud of black ink. No matter what speed, the octopus makes it look effortless and graceful. This says that no matter what speed you are moving, you do so with grace.

Heart

As mentioned earlier, the octopus has three hearts. This means you can divide your heart's intentions into several different areas. It could be that you have several things in your life that require equal attention and love—your partner, your children, your companion animals, a garden. The list may be endless, but you are able to give to each one equally. Another aspect of the octopus in this chakra speaks to its defense mechanism of squirting black ink when it feels threatened. If you want love in your life and this chakra to be opened, review how you react to the world around you to be sure you aren't hiding in your own cloud of fear.

Throat

The octopus doesn't have any organ for hearing or speech; however, they are able to communicate with each other through body language. This suggests that you aren't comfortable using words to communicate your thoughts and feelings, and you prefer to let your actions speak for you. Another aspect of the octopus in this chakra relates to the fact that all species of octopus have venom. This is a caution to choose your words carefully so as not to inflict harm when you do communicate.

Third Eye

Octopuses are thought to be color blind, but their polarized vision is believed to provide the equivalent to adding color to a black and white photo. Recent studies have concluded that cephalopods have photoreceptors in their skin, allowing them to sense light. Most likely, you are psychically very aware most of the time, seeing into a different spectrum than most people. It could also be that you are prone to getting cold shivers on your skin when you are sensing something. As mentioned above, the octopus uses its arms to touch and taste. Instead of blindly trusting your intuition, you like to touch or experience something firsthand before you believe it to be true. This could include exploring meditation practices, reiki, or any other discipline that can't be learned by reading a book.

Crown

The octopus lives in the depths of the ocean. Like many creatures who survive in those realms, the octopus seems otherworldly. You float through the waking world and the dream world with equal comfort, and you typically remember your dreams. Exploring your deepest self is never a challenge for you; in fact, it is where you are most at ease. Most likely, you can go deeper into trance than most people, and it is never a place you feel lost. To you, it feels like home.

OPOSSUM

The opossum has lived on earth for more than seventy million years, making it one of the oldest surviving land mammals. Considered vermin by most due to their tendency to raid garbage cans, opossums are good creatures to have around because not only are they virtually immune to rabies, they also eat disease-carrying ticks. Estimates say that a single opossum can eat as many as five thousand ticks per season. In addition to eating ticks, they also eat roaches, rats, and dead animals, earning them the nickname "nature's little sanitation engineer."

Key Attributes

Strategy, shyness, ability to confuse an opponent, diversion, cleverness, intelligence, and the element of surprise.

Chakra Interpretations

Root

The opossum typically doesn't create its own home; it moves into burrows that have been abandoned by other animals, hollow logs, brush piles, woodpiles, or even human attics. You may have a love of old houses or at least those that have a lived-in feel. Finding a fixer-upper that you can make your own might bring you a lot of joy. Another trait of the opossum is that it doesn't stay in one place for very long, which may mean you don't have any desire to own your own home. You prefer the freedom of being able to move on whenever the urge hits. The opossum is as fastidious as a cat, so even if you do live in an old house, you tend to keep it as clean and germ-free as possible.

Sacral

Because the opossum's tail is prehensile, it can be used almost like a hand. While the opossum can't hang from it, it can be wrapped around tree branches to help with climbing and used for carrying bundles of grasses and other materials. As far as projects or artistic pursuits are concerned, it may be fun for you to think outside the box and try different ways of doing things. If you are right-handed, you might occasionally try using your left just to see if you can or using both hands at the same time. The opossum's hind feet look much like human hands, so you might even try something crazy, such as using your feet to draw or paint. Another aspect of the opossum is that it is a solitary creature, so it is very likely you are too. Your passions are probably more directed toward creative pursuits or work than having intimate connections. Those times that you do seek intimacy are usually for physical release only, and you're okay with that.

Solar Plexus

As mentioned, the opossum can be as fastidious as a cat, especially when it comes to grooming and cleanliness. You may be the kind of person who likes to shower several times a day or who at the very least washes their hands frequently. One of the things an opossum is known for is the ability to fake being dead, which is where we get the expression "playing possum," and it is an involuntary response induced by extreme fear. If something in your life is causing you anxiety to the point where your actions are frozen, I encourage you to seek outside help. Another aspect of the opossum in this chakra may be telling you to trust what is in your gut (pouch), but to make sure you don't hold on to it after it is time to let it go.

Heart

If you have opossum in this chakra, it could mean that events or circumstances in your life have brought you to the point of such extreme hurt or fear that your heart has become frozen. Understandably, some things in life are so hard to handle that shutting down is necessary to survive and heal. Just try to make sure this doesn't become your permanent state of being. At the same time, if this is the case for you, don't go by anyone else's schedule for when you should "get over it"—only you can decide that. Another aspect of the opossum in the heart chakra has to do with an opossum's natural immunity: it's a reminder to not let the actions or words of another hurt your heart, no matter how venomous.

Throat

The opossum in this chakra could mean that speaking or communicating makes you scared stiff, or that you are the kind of person who smiles to hide your fear. If this is the case, try to determine if your fear has a just cause, and if not, take a breath and try to be brave. Another possible meaning has to do with the opossum's diet. As mentioned earlier, they are known for eating very distasteful stuff. This could mean that you are able to take in information that many people can't handle. It may also mean that you are the one who must hear other people's complaints or who has to clean up situational messes that other people make. You don't necessarily enjoy it, but you know it must be done and you know you do it well.

Third Eye

Not only do opossums have poor eyesight, but they don't hear very well either. They depend on their sense of smell for survival. You may have a hard time with traditional meditation or visualization exercises. If this is the case, try adding incense or an essential oil with a pleasing scent to help you tap into your inner sight. Another possibility for the opossum in this chakra is that you don't depend on just what you see to distinguish the truth of a situation. If something doesn't "smell right," trust that instinct; it may be more accurate than your eyes.

Crown

The fact that an opossum spends the first part of its life in momma's pouch offers an illuminating way for you to rebirth your spiritual self. Doing a meditation to help you see the world through the eyes of a young soul could be a profound reawakening. Another possible meaning of the opossum here is that you are fearful of opening to your highest self, so much so that it freezes you with fear. Know that it is where we all come from and where we are all going. Take a breath and try to understand that Spirit loves you and is there to help you.

OTTER

Currently, there are thirteen species of otters living on every continent except Australia and Antarctica. There is some evidence that says the ancestor of the otter existed around twenty-three million years ago but began evolving into the animal we know today around seven million years ago. An amusing fact about the otter comes from Bangladesh, where for centuries fishermen have trained them to act as herders to chase large schools of fish into their nets. Fish herding sure was a new one on me!

Key Attributes

Primal feminine energy, gentleness, faithfulness, playfulness, joy, psychic awareness, having a light heart, sisterhood, deep connection with water, achieving goals with intelligence and clever thinking, and understanding one's inner child.

Chakra Interpretations

Root

Most species of otter live in dens dug into the ground, but the sea otter lives in offshore forests of giant kelp. You probably feel most at home near the water, and like an otter, you are an omnivore but may have a strong preference for seafood, especially shellfish. Otters eat anywhere from 15 to 25 percent of their body weight each day, which means they spend an enormous amount of their day just looking for food. Related to the beaver, the otter will work hard to complete a task. It could be that you work very hard for your living and sometimes feel that you are only working to keep food on the table. One of the best lessons from the otter is how to relax, go with the flow, and not be bogged down by constant work.

Sacral

Otters are highly curious, and sea otters are known to be very creative with tools. This means that you too are probably very curious, and some of your creative outlets include exploration and investigation. If you run into a situation where you don't have the equipment or tool that you need, you just design or build something yourself to do the job. In some belief systems, the otter symbolizes the power of feminine energy, playfulness, joy, and a reminder to have fun in life. This is a reminder that both men and women have their feminine side, and tapping into it can be incredibly healing emotionally. This also says that you can be very sensuous. Not only are you very affectionate with those you love, but you channel your passion into creative energy.

Solar Plexus

Otters are social creatures. Some live in large groups, while others live either alone or with just a few other otters. Either way, except for mating season, otters tend to mostly stay in groups of their own sex. You are probably a very social person but mostly associate with members of your same sex. If you connect more to the sea otter, it may be that you don't do well if you are by yourself for any length of time; you need to be with other people. If you connect more to the river otter, you may be not only solitary but territorial as well. One trait of the otter is that it spends a lot of time grooming; this is essential to its survival. For you, this could mean you lean toward germophobia and feel the need to wash constantly, or it could simply be that you like to look "perfect" before you head out the door.

Heart

As mentioned above, otters are social creatures, but only the giant otter of South America mates for life. Otters have been observed falling asleep holding hands with their partner or with their baby on their chest. While the practical reason for this is so they don't float away, romantically, it might be that you love to spoon with your partner or cuddle with a child while you sleep. If you are single or don't have kids, maybe you snuggle with an animal companion. This also indicates that you are the kind of person who loves with all your heart. You take great pleasure in the success and happiness of others and will do all you can to help anyone who needs it. You can also be very protective and defensive of them.

Throat

Otters are very chatty when among other otters. You probably really enjoy a good gab session with your friends. It could also be that you are part of a big, noisy family whose holiday dinners can get quite loud with laughter and conversation. Outsiders may find it difficult to endure—to them it sounds like noise—but you don't have any trouble keeping up with everything that is being said and wouldn't have it any other way. Another aspect of otter energy says that you put your voice to practical use helping others, especially when it comes to bringing joy back into their lives.

Third Eye

Like cats, otters use their whiskers to sense their environment and to pick up vibrations that come from their prey. They also depend on them when they hunt when it is dark or when water is cloudy. You are one to utilize all your senses and not just your eyes to perceive what is going on around you. You might even get a tingle on your skin that tells you something is up. If this is the case, you should pay attention to it because it is a great natural skill. Another possibility for the otter in this chakra is that some of us can become so somber and bogged down by our self-inflicted limitations or beliefs during spiritual work or meditation practices that nothing can get through. Otter energy is a reminder to let go and find joy in pure exploration.

Crown

Being aquatic, the otter has a natural connection with the subconscious. Most of us have seen photos of otters holding hands while they float on their backs to sleep, but they will also wrap themselves in kelp to keep from floating out to sea. You take precautions when you are doing deep trance work. You go deep but are never in danger of drifting too far. If you connect with otter energy, you might be willing to try meditation using a floatation tank.

OWL

Currently, there are more than two hundred different species of owl that can be found in many types of habitats. Owls have held a variety of symbolic roles, ranging from misfortune and death to prosperity. An interesting fact is that a group of owls is called a *parliament*.

Key Attributes

Deep wisdom and intuitive knowledge, high intelligence, inspiration, independence, introspection, exploration of the unknown, dignity, authority, leadership, confidence, and secrecy.

Chakra Interpretations

Root

Most species of owl live a solitary life and are highly adaptable to different environments and changes. Some owls are very territorial and will fight other owls to defend a claim to their chosen location. Most likely, you can live pretty much anywhere alone, and it could be that you defend your home or your desire to be alone quite adamantly. One possible caution about the owl in this chakra is that it usually swallows its food whole. It could be that you aren't very careful about your diet. You might even tend to eat too fast, which ends up giving you digestive issues. If this is the case for you, take a tip from owl's patience and slow down so you enjoy your food and maybe don't feel ill afterward.

Sacral

Most owls are nocturnal, which says that you prefer to work the night shift or at the very least do your best work after the sun goes down. As far as creative pursuits go, nighttime is when your creativity is at its best, provided you can work in seclusion. An interesting fact about owls is that in most species the female owl is about 25 percent larger than males. Regardless of your actual gender, in your relationship the more feminine half of your partnership might be taller or physically bigger than the more masculine half.

Solar Plexus

With most owls, their coloring and texture tend to mimic their surroundings, allowing them to blend in with the environment, making them nearly invisible. If you so choose, you can be present without being seen. Owls are masters of patience. They watch and wait for the perfect moment before taking any action. You have honed your instincts to razor sharpness and act only when the time is right. Nighttime is when most creatures find shelter because they can't see, but this is the owl's best time. It could be that you are the kind of person who can take what to most people is a disadvantage and turn it into an advantage. The owl preens as soon as it wakes up and will continue to do so throughout the day. If you connect with this feature of the owl, it might take you a long time to get out the door to go anywhere because you probably change your mind about what you are wearing several times or just can't stop tweaking how you look and feel like you need to do "touch-ups" all through the day

Heart

Most owl species are solitary, but a few do mate for life, and which owl you connect to will depend on your life choice. If you are happy living alone but would still like to have companionship, connect with the great horned owl. It stays with one partner, but the pair doesn't nest together. If your desire is to have an affectionate and loving relationship, connect with the barn owl. Barn owls not only nest together, but they also become emotionally attached to their partner and are very cuddly with each other. In fact, barn owls have occasionally been known to die from grief if their mate dies. If remaining solitary is more to your liking, it could be that your heart is devoted to the expansion of knowledge, and very likely this exploration involves things that fall in the realm of the mysterious.

Throat

Other than perhaps the howl of a wolf or coyote, very few noises typify night like the hoot of an owl. Owls are usually silent except when claiming territory or calling to a mate or their chicks. Most likely, you only speak when necessary, for a good reason, and usually with wisdom. An interesting fact is that several species of owl have asymmetrical ears, which means they are positioned at different heights on the owl's head, allowing the owl to pinpoint the location of its prey due to the time difference in which the sound is received in each ear. In keeping with your wisdom and patience, you are one who listens to multiple sides of a situation before you judge what is true.

Third Eye

One of the most striking features of an owl is its eyes. Owls can see in three dimensions and have binocular vision like humans, but unlike humans, their eyes are not *eyeballs*: they are cylindrical and completely immobile. To compensate, an owl can turn its head approximately 270 degrees from right to left and almost completely upside down. If you don't understand something at first glance, you will turn it over and examine it from as many different angles as it takes until you do. A possible downside is that you are so focused on understanding details that you miss the big picture. Not only do you view things from a different perspective, but you use your inborn filters to see through various layers and may even be able to see different light spectrums and into the spirit world.

Crown

For you, dream time can be particularly potent. If you aren't already lucid dreaming, you might want to try practicing it. In some cultures, the owl represents magic, prophecy, and reincarnation. It may be that you have memories of a previous life, and through meditation, you may be able to trigger memories of that life or find clarity. One of the most striking characteristics of an owl is the disklike shape of its face, which the owl can alter using facial muscles so that it acts like a radar dish funneling sound to its ears. Try using these attributes to focus and develop your own radar by visualizing your own face as that of an owl.

PORCUPINE

The porcupine's name is a derivative of the Medieval French *porc espin*, which means "spiny pig." Like otters, porcupines are very loving, curious, and playful creatures, but they also have a well-known defense they can use if they feel threatened. The sharp quills, as many as thirty thousand, that they are so famous for are mixed in with fur on their back, sides, and tail. The rest of their body is soft hair. Porcupines fall into two groups: Old World and New World. Old World porcupines live in southern Europe, Asia, and Africa, and New World porcupines live in North America and the northern part of South America. Like beavers, porcupines live in forests, where they eat mostly wood and bark, but they also like some plants and fruit. Contrary to popular belief, porcupines can't shoot their quills, but they do detach relatively easily, as many family dogs painfully discover.

Key Attributes

Childlike innocence, maintaining a sense of curiosity and wonder, adaptability, a reminder to not let other people's opinions affect you, facing your fears, and having faith and trust.

Chakra Interpretations

Root

North American porcupines prefer to live in forests but can adapt to live in harsher environments. Most likely, you are the kind of person who would rather spend time in the woods than go to the beach. You may even like having a house surrounded by trees. The fact that the porcupine sleeps during the day and comes out at night to find food could mean that you tend wake up in the middle of the night to raid the fridge. Another aspect speaks of the porcupine's preference for living a simple life. You don't need a fancy home to make you feel safe and happy. The porcupine moves through life at its own pace. You don't let anyone push you to do anything you don't want to do, nor can anyone rush you. From a work perspective, it is probably best if you can be on flex time because if you are required to punch a clock at a particular time, it will always be a struggle.

Sacral

Porcupines are primarily nocturnal, so night could be the time when you wake up and are at your most energetic and creative. New World porcupines are excellent climbers and spend a lot of time in trees. However, they occasionally fall because they see something tempting just out of reach, and they can't help but try to grasp it. You are not afraid to stretch your limits, even if you fail. It is more important to you to test yourself and see just how far you can go. Another possibility has to do with porcupines being observed standing on their hind legs doing a rhythmic dance. No one is exactly sure why they do it—possibly stress, maybe a mating dance, maybe to relax, or just because they like it. It could be that when you are anxious or bored, it is hard for you to be still. You rock from foot to foot or pace around the room.

Solar Plexus

An obvious feature of the porcupine is its quills; they scare people. For the most part, you have a happy-go-lucky personality and may exude a gentle, playful nature, but there may be something about you that frightens people. It takes a lot, such as a direct attack, to get you riled up, but you are perfectly capable of defending yourself, and when you do, it is in ways that will have your attacker thinking twice before ever crossing you again. If you are exuding a prickly aura due to fear, porcupine energy could be telling you that your shields and defenses are too thick. It may be time to learn to trust so you don't miss out on the beautiful experiences and joy that are available to you. It might surprise people to find out how cuddly you are.

Heart

Porcupines have a gentle nature and a live-and-let-live approach to life, but they aren't very social. It is possible that because of past hurts, you keep people away. Another possibility in this chakra has to do with the porcupine having a childlike wonder. On the surface, people might think of you as cantankerous, but once they get to know you, they discover that you're sweet and full of playfulness and joy. The critical question is, do you know this about yourself?

Throat

Porcupines rely a great deal on scent to communicate. This may mean that you like to leave a trail of your fragrance behind as you walk through a room so people know that you have been there. Another possibility is that porcupines are vocal. Most of us have seen videos of cute porcupines mumbling over a piece of food. It could be that you tend to talk to yourself or mumble and make odd vocal noises while you're eating or busy with a project or activity. A word of caution would be to make sure you don't combine your vocalizations with your quills. It probably takes a lot to get you to the point where you feel like you must use them, but your barbs can inflict a lot of damage.

Third Eye

Porcupines tend to be nearsighted. It could be that you only trust what is right in front of you and you are not comfortable with expanding your worldview. Porcupine energy encourages you to see beyond your guarded perception and explore the realm of the unknown with a childlike wonder. You never know what kind of tasty treats you might discover. Another aspect of the porcupine in this chakra is dependence on other senses. You need additional input beyond just what you can see before you trust a situation.

Crown

Porcupine in this chakra could be saying that apprehension and fear of the unknown may be keeping you from connecting with your highest self or with Spirit. As mentioned already, porcupines have been observed dancing. Trance or ritual dancing is or could be a way for you to connect with Spirit. If you don't already attend them, try going to drumming events, trance dances, or celebrations with a bonfire. At the very least, you'll have a blast.

RABBIT

Beliefs about the rabbit range from symbolizing good fortune in China to being known as *Fear Caller* by some Native Americans. In Celtic tradition, the rabbit or hare is associated with the Otherworld. During the Renaissance, artists used rabbits to represent both purity and lust. Because of their prolific reproductive nature, it is not surprising that they became a symbol of fertility, the season of spring and rebirth, and eventually Easter. Today the rabbit has also become a symbol for cruelty-free products, making it easier for those who try to only buy products that are not tested on animals. Rabbits can be litter-box trained and make excellent house pets. Because they are social by nature, they make great companions not only for the humans in the house but also the other pets. Many people think giving a baby bunny to a child for Easter is cute; unfortunately, however, many of these well-meaning gifts end up in animal shelters or worse before their first birthday. It is much better to give a toy bunny, but if a real one is genuinely wanted, shelters typically have several available for adoption.

Key Attributes

Creative intuition, gentleness, possibly obsessive thoughts about fear and loss, a guide to the shadow world, ability to attract abundance, and fertility.

Chakra Interpretations

Root

Rabbits are very territorial and live in hierarchical groups that often overlap with other groups. They are social creatures and need companionship and community. These aspects could be symbolizing that you don't need or want much alone time. In fact, it could be that you are uncomfortable spending any time alone. You may even like to live with housemates if you don't live in a traditional family structure. Another possibility for the rabbit in the root chakra has to do with how a rabbit constructs its warren. It builds the warren not only with different rooms but also multiple underground tunnels with many entrances and exits. You probably feel safest if you have various places you can run to if you feel threatened.

Sacral

One well-known adage is "breeding like rabbits." If this speaks to you, it could mean that you either already have or dream of having lots of children. If human children are not what you desire, perhaps you fill your home with lots of companion animals. You might very well be a crazy cat person. Rabbits can go from being very calm to frantic in the blink of an eye and are adept at staying hidden when they want to, and if this speaks to you, it could be that you are the kind of person who can disappear in a crowd or party if they feel uncomfortable. You can also go from sleeping to wide awake and functional right away, even without coffee.

Solar Plexus

The Fear Caller aspect of the rabbit may be saying that you have a knee-jerk reaction when it comes to what frightens you. You might have a habit of running for safety at the slightest twinge of fear. Fear is thought, and thoughts have energy. The universe doesn't know the difference between things you want and things you don't, only that you are sending out energy. This is a reminder and a caution that you might be attracting the very thing you fear, and it may be holding you back from truly living. Try cloaking yourself in bravery so the projections can stop. On the other hand, a happy rabbit performs a cute dance called a binky: you might be the kind of person who literally jumps for joy when they are happy!

Heart

As mentioned earlier, rabbits need the company of others. Rabbit energy says that your heart only feels safe and happy when you are among others of like mind so you can let your shields down. Another possibility has to do with rabbits not being monogamous. It is possible that being with just one person isn't a high priority for you; in fact, you might even be polyamorous. Regardless of which rings true, you love and need to snuggle on a regular basis.

Throat

Rabbits tend to be quiet creatures, but they do make some noises, including cooing, honking, teeth grinding (a happy sound), and even growling like a cat. It might be that you tend to be a shy person but will give a quiet warning if you feel challenged or threatened. It could also be that you are afraid of your own voice or even have stage fright. If this is the case, try to be brave and speak your truth.

Third Eye

Baby rabbits are born naked and blind and need to remain in a fur-lined nest for the first few days of their lives. This part of rabbit life could be saying that you are afraid of opening your third eye to what is unfamiliar, preferring to stay in the safety of the known. If you want to be more open in this chakra, try calling on the energy of an animal whose courage you admire. Once a rabbit is an adult, it is farsighted to the extreme, and it has a blind spot in front of its nose. This could be saying that you perceive a great deal but sometimes miss the obvious.

Crown

When you are in prayer or meditating, you do so from a place of stillness and humility. If not, the rabbit in this chakra is a suggestion to try this approach. Being quiet and listening carefully to what is going on in your surroundings, you can hear with the rabbit's large ears the messages that are coming through for you. Another possibility is the previously mentioned Fear Caller aspect. It is possible that the concept of Spirit is too big and scary for you to grasp, so you shy away from it. There is no reason to fear: Spirit loves you and wants a connection with you.

RACCOON

In addition to its mask, the raccoon is known for its dexterous front paws. The scientific name, *Procyon lotor*, is Neo-Latin and translates to "before-dog washer," and the English word *raccoon* comes from Proto-Algonquian and means "animal that scratches with its hands." In fact, if you look up the translation for *raccoon* in nearly any language, the meaning is almost the same. Raccoons usually prefer to live in a wooded area, but their habitat has expanded over time to include even highly populated human areas. It helps that raccoons are quite adaptable in their housing choices. They are known for stealing food from trash cans and bird feeders and will even sneak into people's homes. If caught in the act, raccoons usually have a "so what?" response, but if provoked, they can become vicious.

Key Attributes

Understanding the nature of masks, disguises, resourcefulness, dexterity, shape-shifting, secrecy, curiosity, cleverness, playfulness, adaptability, and working with one's hands.

Chakra Interpretations

Root

While preferring to live in wooded areas near water, raccoons have adjusted to urban life out of necessity because of shrinking habitat. It is possible that in a perfect world you would have a quiet house in the woods near a babbling brook. The reality might be that you live in a more urban setting, but you are perfectly content there as well. Because they are opportunistic eaters, one possibility for raccoon in this chakra could be you aren't particularly fussy or careful about what you eat. In fact, some might classify your diet as consisting mostly of garbage.

Sacral

The hands of a raccoon are incredible. They have many times more touch receptors in their front paws than in their hind feet, and a significant portion of the processing space in a raccoon's brain is dedicated to those front paws. This attribute could be a very beneficial symbol for you, especially if you are in a healing art that requires the use of your hands, such as chiropractic, massage therapy, or even reiki or light weaving. Since most of a raccoon's time is spent searching for food, it could be that one of your creative passions is cooking or baking. Other creative possibilities could be mask making, working with clay, or even being an actor.

Solar Plexus

The raccoon wears a natural mask. Very simply, this is saying that you don multiple masks depending on the situation. It could be you are one person at work, another when you are with others of like mind, and yet another when you are alone. Maybe you feel like this is just what is necessary to feel safe. It could also be that you haven't yet discovered who you are and are trying on different masks to find out. All are valid approaches to living; just don't wear yourself out in the process. It might be helpful for you to do some mirror meditation work to discover the mask you wear when you look at yourself.

Heart

Though historically thought to be solitary, raccoons seem to like to stay in small groups with members of the same sex. It is likely that you are most comfortable having a small group of very close friends of your same gender. You may even acquire a new group of friends every few years. You might be perfectly fine as a loner, but even you have times when you like having someone else in your life, though only if they respect your boundaries and need for occasional solitude.

Throat

Some researchers think that raccoons make up to two hundred different sounds, and many of those sounds can be mistaken for other animals. Fighting raccoons sound like fighting cats, their screams sound like those of a screech owl, and baby raccoons, coincidently called kittens, are known to purr and mew. Most likely, you communicate in a variety of ways depending on the situation at hand. Raccoons are usually easygoing but will stand their ground when the circumstances call for it. You tend to have a high threshold of annoyance but will growl if someone pushes the wrong buttons.

Third Eye

Raccoons spend a lot of time in trees because they can observe their environment and watch for potential danger. You are someone who looks at things from a higher perspective. Raccoons have poor eyesight, so they depend on their sense of smell. They also use their hands to thoroughly investigate an object. To you, something isn't real unless you can touch it. This belief could be keeping you from opening this chakra fully. There are some theories that suggest the raccoon's mask helps them with night vision by reducing glare. It may be useful for you to try wearing a sleep mask when you meditate so no light or glare can get through to distract you.

Crown

A raccoon's magic is its mask, which can be translated to shape-shifting and mask wearing in a ritual or shamanic setting. Transforming yourself is a well-established way to reach a higher state of consciousness. If mask wearing is not already a part of your spiritual practice, the raccoon in this chakra could be a suggestion to add it. As mentioned above, another suggestion is to wear a sleep mask during trance work to keep any glare or light from distracting you.

RAVEN

Ravens are thought by some to be the smartest of all birds. They use tools and are capable of solving complicated problems using reasoning skills. They will sometimes work with other ravens and even barter to get what they want. Ravens often mimic the calls of other birds, and they can learn human speech better than some parrots. Because its beak can't break open a carcass, it will imitate the call of a predator to attract one to the prey to do it for the raven. A great deal of often conflicting lore and mythology surrounds the raven. Some portray them as being mischievous or an evil omen, but others depict them in a positive light. Some view the raven as a messenger of the gods. In Britain, legend says at least six ravens must be in residence at the Tower of London or the country will fall.

Key Attributes

Keeper of secrets, introspection, imagination, courage, dignity, self-knowledge, healing, shape-shifting, a messenger from the spirit world, magic, confronting fears, and achieving one's goals with intelligence and planning.

Chakra Interpretations

Root

Ravens can be found living in a wide variety of habitats across western and northern North America, including deciduous and evergreen forests, snowy areas, high desert, sea coast, and a variety of other places. This means you can probably adapt to living pretty much anywhere. Since ravens aren't as social as crows, you do fine on your own, but you do equally well in a small community or with a life mate. While adult ravens mate for life, juvenile ravens fly around in gangs. They don't do this to cause trouble but for security reasons and to better their chances of finding food. It very well could be that in your teen years you had a close-knit group of friends that laid a foundation for the person you are today, and it is entirely possible that some of those connections became lifelong friendships.

Sacral

Ravens are highly creative and love to play both by themselves and with other ravens. They have been known to make toys using sticks, pine cones, or whatever they can find. The raven symbolizes that you are highly intelligent, curious, and creative. You probably love figuring out puzzles or problems. You might even dabble in inventing things. Ravens living in colder climates have been witnessed rolling in snow like dogs do. It could be that you love being out in the snow. You might be an avid skier or love to snowshoe. Maybe you enjoy building snowmen with your kids. Whatever you get involved in, you approach it with humor, and sharing your findings or creations brings you great joy. If you're working too hard, raven energy is telling you to get out and play.

Solar Plexus

Ravens are very confident, inquisitive birds and symbols of the unknown in many cultures. As mentioned already, you might be the kind of person who likes to figure out a puzzle. What you may not realize is that because you carry yourself with an aura of mystery, to other people you are an enigma that they can't quickly figure out. New people you meet may be in awe of and perhaps even a little intimidated by you, but those in your inner circle know the real you—even your trickster side.

Heart

Ravens are empathetic. They have been known to comfort a fellow raven that has lost a fight and mourn when a member of their flock dies. You might often be the one to reach out to a family member or friend during times of crisis, and it could even be that you do this for your profession. Your wisdom keeps you grounded, so you don't take on another's pain while your heart feels and comforts. Another aspect is that ravens mate for life. If this is the case for you, you are truly blessed. You have a partner who equals you in every way: in intelligence, wit, humor, and the capacity for love. If you haven't yet found your life mate, don't settle for anything less.

Throat

Ravens have incredibly sophisticated vocal capabilities, and their call can be heard up to a mile away. As mentioned above, ravens are very empathetic. Your combination of intelligence and compassion means that you can use your voice for the benefit of others, even over long distances. It could be that you counsel people remotely via the web. Your confidence says that you can make yourself not only heard but heeded. Another aspect of the raven in this chakra is in connection with their mimicking: you could be good at improvisation or imitation, much to the entertainment of your friends and family. In addition to sound, ravens also use gesture to communicate, so there is a good chance that you talk with your hands.

Third Eye

Ravens have large forebrains that help with logical thinking, memory, and vision. You take in the aspects of any situation very quickly and precisely, allowing you to act if need be. One possible meaning for the raven in this chakra is that you have a near photographic memory for faces, anything you've read, or remembering directions to a place even if you have only been there once. Since ravens can see both polarized and ultraviolet light, another possible interpretation is that, in addition to seeing the *real* world clearly, you may be able to see things others don't, such as auras or the spirit world.

Crown

In many cultures, the raven is considered the keeper of secrets. Sometimes our subconscious knows things that our conscious mind tends to block. Raven in this chakra says that through meditation and introspection, you can bring down those blocks and tap into your inner secrets. In keeping with the raven's social nature, it could be that you like working with meditation or prayer groups. It could be that you have a meditative practice with your life partner. Whichever is true, raven calls you to explore realms of mystery, be it on your own or with others.

SALMON

Fossil records that date from nearly seven million years ago show a fish known as the *sabertooth salmon*, and researchers in Alaska have discovered evidence that Ice Age humans ate salmon. In the Pacific Northwest, the Chinook salmon is a keystone species because it supports over a hundred other species, including the orca, the bear, the river otter, the eagle, and many others. Druid tradition considers the salmon sacred and the oldest and wisest of all creatures. Celtic myth speaks of the Salmon of Knowledge, and some Native American tribes perform salmon dances to honor the salmon for sacrificing its life.

Key Attributes

Ancient wisdom, returning home to regenerate, the rebirth of spiritual knowledge, overcoming obstacles, achieving goals with determination and confidence, and genetic memory.

Chakra Interpretations

Root

Salmon live in the northern Atlantic and Pacific Oceans as well as some inland lakes. Salmon are what is called *anadromous* because they live in both fresh and salt water. Most are born in fresh water, migrate to the sea, and then return to fresh water to reproduce. One truth about the salmon has to do with their instinct-driven determination. Their connection with home is so powerful; they can smell the one stream where they hatched and will return to it in a few years, sometimes traveling thousands of miles to get there. This unbreakable bond with their birthplace says returning home to regenerate is necessary for your very survival. This might mean your ancestral home or your current home. Regardless, no matter how far you roam, getting *home* is what drives you. Another possibility with this chakra is that exploring ancestor work and finding your roots may be quite insightful and healing for you.

Sacral

In many myths and legends, the salmon represents the attainment of knowledge. It is possible that you are passionate about learning, be it something new or even ancient wisdom. As mentioned above, a salmon acts with a singular determination. They forego food during migration, so sadly this means that many don't survive once they reach their destination. This possibility might be a warning for you not to get so caught up in your passions or work that you forget to take care of yourself and your basic needs. Don't let what drives you end up killing you!

Solar Plexus

Most fish would die if they moved between salt and fresh water the way the salmon does, but it survives due to very efficient osmoregulation. This allows the salmon to literally control how its body functions between the two environments. The salmon in this chakra says wherever you find yourself, no matter how alien or extreme the differences in setting, you adapt. Parallel to this is the fact that most species of salmon are one color when they are young but then change color when they are ready to spawn. If this doesn't represent the need to change to adapt to a situation, it could simply be that you like to change up your wardrobe or even your hair color on a seasonal basis; this helps make you feel renewed. If something is in the salmon's way, it will simply jump over it. This aspect speaks to you having the ability to find unique ways to solve challenging problems. In situations where most people only see barriers, you find your way around them or over them. Salmon energy also says that even when the journey is arduous, your uncanny instincts guide you; you always know where you're going and how to get there.

Heart

As mentioned in the root chakra, it may also be that home is what matters most to your heart and getting there as often as possible is what drives you. The word *salmon* is thought to come from the Latin *salire,* which means "to leap." In this chakra, the salmon may be saying that you are the kind of person who literally jumps for joy when they are happy. Another aspect acknowledges that while you may have a tough exterior, inwardly you are tender-hearted and easily hurt. Embrace your experiences as lessons rather than hardships; each one adds to your stockpile of wisdom.

Throat

There are many legends about salmon being a source of great wisdom. You are very mindful of how you communicate, be it verbally or written, and you do so with forethought and wisdom. Another possibility could be that it is time for you to share your knowledge with others. You might become a teacher, give a workshop, or share your experiences in poetry, song or storytelling. There is a reason you have had the life experiences that you've had, and others may be able to learn from them.

Third Eye

In this chakra, salmon energy says you have wisdom and knowledge beyond your years. It may be that you're not even sure from where this knowledge comes. In some cases, it could be a soul or past-life memory, or you might be accessing the knowledge of your ancestors or possibly your Akashic records. The source doesn't matter—just learn to trust it. A suggestion is to take a pilgrimage or inward spiritual journey to find clarity and rejuvenation. Your life may never be the same.

Crown

In addition to being guided by smell, the salmon is guided by the earth's magnetic field. It is thought young salmon imprint the magnetic location of their home river and are guided by it later in life. The salmon in this chakra could be a suggestion to see if there are connections to your spiritual side that you learned early in life but can't remember with your conscious mind. Maybe you had a spirit guide as a child but were told they didn't exist and you were forced to forget them. If any memories like this are in you lying dormant, waiting to be tapped, you can find them again if you take a leap of faith, let go of your surface thoughts, and dive deep. Salmon energy will help you overcome any obstacle to reach your goal of enlightenment.

SEAL

Like other marine mammals, seals were once land animals that moved into the sea millions of years ago. Seals belong to a group of animals called *pinnipeds*, meaning "fin-footed." Currently, thirty-three different pinniped species can be found around the world, nineteen of which are members of the seal species. Seals are divided into two families: seals with ears, like sea lions and fur seals, and seals without ears, like the common or true seal. While seals spend most of their time in the water, they gather together on land in large, noisy social groups called *colonies* to sunbathe, mate, and raise their young.

Key Attributes

Lucid dreaming, protection from danger, creativity, imagination, sensuality, curiosity, intuition, and being at home in your own body.

Chakra Interpretations

Root

As mentioned above, when they are on land, be it on rocks or the beach, seals gather in large, noisy groups. If you connect with the seal in this chakra, you are happiest and feel safest when you are around big groups of people, and the louder and more chaotic sounding the better. Since seals can be found living in both warm and cold climates (but most of them prefer the cold), it could be that you can live anywhere but prefer more northern climates. This could also mean that when you go on vacation, rather than going somewhere warm, you head for the snow. Seals are carnivores and eat mostly fish, but they will eat any meat that comes out of the water. This says it is likely that you have a fondness for any kind of seafood and possibly even for sushi.

Sacral

Seals appear to struggle while they are on dry land, but in water they have total freedom of movement. Seal energy may be asking you if you struggle with being at home in your body. If you can let go of whatever is weighing you down, you'll be able to swim through life more comfortably. Another aspect is that in the wild, males especially can quickly go from being calm to viciously fighting over a female or territory. You might have a hair-trigger temper and are not even aware of it, which can be scary and confusing to those around you. If this is the case for you, when something upsets you, before you react, practice taking a moment to breathe or just walk away from the situation. Those around you will be grateful.

Solar Plexus

Not many people know that seals shed their skin once a year, and this may be the source of the myth that seals can become a human. You enjoy changing your appearance, possibly on an annual basis, trying something like getting a new hairstyle or color, updating your wardrobe, or wearing makeup differently. If this rings true for you, doing so makes you feel like a new person who can take on the world. As mentioned above, seals, especially males, can become very territorial and will fight with others. When people see you, they may see sweet, gentle eyes, but don't let them forget that you are perfectly willing and able to guard and protect what you value. Yet another possibility, not associated with your exterior, is that it is very likely that you have a deep connection to your inner rhythms, and you know who you are even without shedding your outer skin.

Heart

Seals are at home both on land and in the water, and they are natural-born swimmers. Most likely, you are a balanced person, in touch with your emotions but also grounded. You have a carefree outlook on life and stay joyful and playful. Even when you do get angry, you are quick to apologize and calm down rapidly from whatever upset you. Most likely, people are happy to see you and tend to smile and laugh more when you're around. Since seals don't stay with a mate, most likely you are devoted to a child, but not necessarily a spouse. "Child" in this case could mean an actual human child, but it could also mean a companion animal, a garden, or even a project. Point being, you give of yourself to something else and are not self-centered.

Throat

On land, a seal can hear up to four octaves of sound, but in the water, they can hear up to seven. You are the kind of person who doesn't just rely on what you hear, but you also listen to the emotions beneath what someone is saying. When you see a group of seals on land sunning themselves, it can get very noisy. You might feel like you need to talk louder than everyone else just to be heard. It could also be that you have a group of friends or family that all talk at the same time. For you, this means *home,* and you wouldn't want it any other way.

Third Eye

Seals have incredibly dark and mysterious eyes. It is easy to see why many traditions believed that a human was hiding under the seal's skin. On land, a seal's eyesight is not that great, but in the water it is far superior to a human's. A seal's whiskers, known as *vibrissae*, are very sensitive, can move independently, and the seal uses them to ascertain their surroundings and to detect prey. These sensitivities are telling you that you have two powerful tools to help you explore your subconscious. Not only can your mind's eye see clearly, but your external sensors can detect changes in energy as well.

Crown

Seals can sleep either on land or in the water. So that they can continue breathing while in water, they sleep in a position called *bottling*, which means their whole body is underwater, but their head is exposed, like a bottle bobbing in the water. Like other marine mammals, if seals are sleeping in the water, only half their brain sleeps while the other half stays alert for danger. However, if they are sleeping on land, their whole brain rests, even reaching REM sleep. The seal in this chakra could mean that when you meditate, you fully relax even though half your brain is aware of everything going on around you.

SKUNK

Skunks are beautiful, shy, nocturnal creatures that are very distinguishable, even from a great distance. Similar to the porcupine, the skunk has a reputation that is not based on physical aggression but on a defense mechanism that everyone knows. Naturally fearless and calm, they will only spray if provoked or spooked. Since spraying renders them helpless until their bodies can develop more musk, skunks will first try a series of warnings intended to intimidate an attacker, including stomping the ground. In the case of the tiny spotted skunk, the animal does a silly-looking handstand dance. One interesting fact is that the skunk is resistant to the bite of the rattlesnake and the stings of both bees and scorpions, and it will happily eat them all.

Key Attributes

The power of respect, reputation, self-esteem, inner vision, playfulness, trust, aggression only when provoked, being true to yourself, solitude, and self-reliance.

Chakra Interpretations

Root

Skunks are very adaptable and can thrive in many different habitats, but they will rarely venture beyond two miles from their den. Most likely, you are not particular about where you choose to live, but you don't like living too far away from civilization; you prefer living somewhere within a quick drive or walk to grocery stores. It might even be that in your adult life you decide to live in or close to the neighborhood where you grew up. A skunk's diet tends to change based on availability and the seasons. It could be that you like visiting your local farmers market to gather whatever is in season. A downside and a word of caution:

since the skunk isn't a very picky eater, be sure your diet doesn't consist of mostly garbage.

Sacral

The skunk's strongest sense is smell. The animal spends a lot of time with its nose to the ground, and it is an incredibly curious creature. This combination could mean that you have a passion for research and rarely lift your nose up from a book or your work. It could also mean that your sense of smell is more acute than most people's. For some people, this can be a problem when out in public, but if you can turn it into a positive and make a career from it, there are several professional possibilities, such as chef, sommelier, and even professional perfumer. Given that skunks are nocturnal, the hours between dusk and dawn are probably when you are your most productive and creative.

Solar Plexus

The skunk is the ultimate pacifist. You desire a peaceful existence and for the most part have an easygoing, live-and-let-live approach to life, but like the skunk, your self-defense may be legendary. While you are usually a calm person, at the same time people know they should never cross or startle you. If they do, you defend yourself without causing physical harm but leave your adversary sorry for their action. This could also be a warning to ask yourself if your boundaries are too strong and if this in turn is keeping others from getting close to you. One of the skunk's primary lessons is that of respect: how to expect it from others but also how to give it in return. You are probably good at knowing how to welcome people with kindness but also how to tell them to keep their distance without feelings getting hurt. Skunk energy says you know who you are; you walk your talk and live authentically, regardless of the opinions of others.

Heart

Skunks are solitary creatures with no social structure. You may prefer to keep others at a distance and will sometimes defend your solitude in unpleasant ways. Skunks have a gentle and playful nature, and it could very well be that you are self-entertaining and don't feel lonely just because there isn't anyone around. You probably do fine with just companion animals. The skunk's obvious defense could be asking if this is how you want your heart to be perceived. If not, try lowering your shields.

Throat

To ward off a predator, the skunk will communicate that it is upset by stamping its feet. This says you might have a bit of a temper and may even be a foot stomper. Anyone who crosses you should be happy that you give an outward warning because the next stage of your anger isn't pleasant. Other noises a skunk makes include hissing and clicking its teeth. It might be that instead of stomping your feet, you tend to grit your teeth and swallow your words. If this is the case, skunk energy urges you to speak up for yourself. Don't depend on your reputation alone to speak for you.

Third Eye

Skunks have very poor eyesight and can only see what is right in front of them. It could be that you have a scientific or logical view of the world, especially for things that science hasn't yet been able to prove. It might be that you question anything beyond your three-dimensional existence. The skunk in this chakra could be urging you to take off the blinders and learn to explore the mysterious. On the opposite side of this, you could be the kind of person who, when examining the unknown, does so with a singular focus and ignores everything and everyone around them. If this is the case, the skunk reminds you to take in the whole forest and not just concentrate on a single leaf.

Crown

The calm gentleness of the nocturnal skunk says that when you enter the realm of spirit, you do so from a position of curiosity. Your humbleness says that you approach the sacred from a respectful yet fearless posture. Since it is your nature to be solitary, you don't feel the need to do mystical work within a group structure; the connection you have with Spirit is a private one and not something you have any desire or need to share.

SNAKE

The snake is one of the most ancient of all mythological creatures and one whose meaning differs drastically depending on culture and belief. To some, the snake represents the face of evil, but to others, it represents fertility and wisdom. Still others link it to creation, healing energy, and transformation. Throughout the world, many cultures use representations of snakes as guardians for their temples. Due to their venom, snakes have a connection to poisons and medicine. Modern medicine uses the caduceus (two snakes wrapped around a staff, plus a set of wings) as a symbol for healing, but some believe a more authentic medical symbol is the staff of Asclepius (one snake wrapped around a staff), who was the deity of medicine and healing arts in Greek mythology.

Key Attributes

Death, rebirth, transformation, primordial life energy, respect, sexuality, healing, spiritual wisdom, silence, and occult knowledge.

Chakra Interpretations

Root

Snakes move along the ground and stay connected with the earth's energy. You have a connection to these forces that you feel to your very core. Another aspect of snake speaks to its need for heat. You probably aren't a fan of cold weather climates. Summer may be your favorite season, and you can think of nothing more relaxing than basking in the sun. Another aspect of snake in the root chakra says that you may be at the start of a powerful life transformation, a time when you are shedding an old skin and beginning a new phase of your life. If this is the case, your transformation will be down to the cellular level, and this new life will be like being reborn.

Sacral

In many cultures, snakes are associated with both male and female sexuality and are something to be honored and not feared. The snake says you are very sensuous and passionate about all things in life. Some snakes kill their prey by wrapping their bodies around it and squeezing it to death; this is a caution to make sure you aren't acting in such a possessive way to the people in your life that they feel suffocated. A long shot, but the shedding aspect of the snake in this chakra brings up a possibility that will only apply to a very few: you may be in the process of transforming your sexual or gender identity. If this is the case, snake energy supports your transformation and wants you to honor it and be true to who you are deep inside.

Solar Plexus

The scales that cover a snake's body are made of the same material as human fingernails, keratin. Not only do you know who you are, but you can protect yourself from external pressures to be something different. Your preference is to be left alone. While you aren't one to instigate aggression, you have no problem striking quickly if the need arises. Another aspect of the snake in the solar plexus chakra speaks to the fact that the head of a decapitated venomous snake can still bite up to an hour after it has died. Not only do you not back down from a battle, but you keep going, sometimes viciously, long after the fight should be over. If this is the case for you, a valuable lesson is to know when it is time to accept defeat. It doesn't mean failure; it is just time for you to move on.

Heart

Snakes need to warm themselves in the sun in order to move or even to eat. The snake in this chakra could be asking if your heart has become frozen. Regardless of how much your heart has suffered, the snake's powerful transformation and healing can help you shed old pains and rebirth the love within you. Another possibility could be if you are in a difficult relationship, it might be time to shed that skin and slither away.

Throat

A snake flicks its tongue to smell the air. If you connect with snake in this chakra, you might be the kind of person who investigates a situation fully before you speak, and you do so in unconventional ways. Just be sure that when you do speak, your words are not full of venom. Unless of course the situation calls for it, in which case your quarry has crossed the wrong person. One caution is that some venomous snakes have been known to accidentally die from biting themselves, though rarely; be mindful that your words don't come back to bite you. One more aspect from a practical perspective is that a snake swallows its prey whole, so remember to chew your food.

Third Eye

Snakes don't have eyelids; they have a single transparent scale called a *brille* that protects each eye. This symbolizes that it is possible that you are walking around with this chakra open and may not even be aware of it. One sign of this would be if you feel uncomfortable in a crowd or feel like you are picking up other people's thoughts. If this is the case, you are too psychically open and may need to practice some shielding meditations. On the flip side of this, this chakra could be wide open by choice and you are entirely comfortable with that. Like the lizard, you could have been born with this chakra open and have never known any different. Additionally, snakes don't have external ears; they sense vibrations in their skin and throughout their bodies. If you are prone to cold chills or shivers for no apparent reason, you might be picking up messages or place memory. It is not something to fear; it is a gift you were born with and is well worth honing. You might be surprised what you can discover.

Crown

A snake's ability to transform itself might be saying that you are in the process of changing your spiritual practice or are starting to develop a new one. If you have been feeling like you are ready to shed outgrown beliefs about yourself, your connection to Spirit, or the world around you, the snake is an excellent ally to have. You might find the answers you seek by participating in something like a vision quest or a spiritual retreat so that you can emerge transformed.

SPIDER

Spiders are surrounded by a wide array of myths and superstitions. Some see them as evil, others see them as symbols of creation and the sacred feminine, and still others believe they bring wealth and good fortune. Spiders are vital to a healthy ecosystem because they eat more harmful insects than birds and bats eat combined. Spiders are also a food source for many small mammals, birds, and fish. The silk in a spiderweb is five times stronger than a strand of steel of the same thickness. In fifteenth-century Italy, it was believed that the bite of a tarantula spider caused a form of hysteria that could only be cured by doing a frenzied dance called the *tarantella*. Perhaps the "dance" some people do today due to arachnophobia stems from a genetic memory of this.

Key Attributes

Creation, weaver of the web of life, honoring the sacred, infinity, teacher of language, intelligence, creativity, feminine energy, receptivity, patience, and facing one's darker self.

Chakra Interpretations

Root

Spiders can adapt to life pretty much anywhere. You probably aren't very particular about where you live, and you can make due with whatever is available. The spiderweb is an engineering marvel; created from the silk produced by the spider's own body, it is remarkably resilient while still being incredibly delicate. You might dream of building your own house with your own hands. Another trait of the spider is that when it walks, it always has four legs on the ground, meaning you are very good at remaining grounded and balanced.

Sacral

In Druid lore, the spider is not only a weaver but the teacher of language. For you, writing could be a powerful creative passion. If you aren't already, start writing down stories, poems, thoughts, or ideas. Maybe it is time for you to start a blog or to keep a dream journal. Another creative outlet would be weaving, knitting, or crocheting, especially if you spin your own yarn. A not-so-flattering aspect of spider in this chakra comes from the belief that a female spider sometimes cannibalizes her mate after sex. This could be a caution that your partner may be feeling devoured by you, or that you are the one being devoured. It could also mean that to you sex is just a release, and you have no real feelings toward your partner. That's okay if both parties agree to the arrangement ahead of time. If not, someone will get hurt.

Solar Plexus

A spider's legs are covered in tiny hairs called *trichobothria* that pick up vibrations in the air, which allows them to sense when potential prey is approaching or if there is a predator they need to avoid. Your instincts are incredibly receptive to the point where you might have difficulty being in groups of people because you are unconsciously picking up their thoughts and energies. If this is the case, try practice shielding exercises so that nothing unwelcome comes through. One more aspect of the spider in this chakra says you prefer to work on your own rather than in a team situation. You do your most creative work when you can be left alone. It is not uncommon for you to surprise people with something beautiful that you have created seemingly out of thin air.

Heart

In some cultures, spiders are creators of the universe and are also depicted as destroyers. In other cultures, spiders are the weavers of fate. The spider in this chakra is a reminder that we often create many of the situations in which we find ourselves. Are you the weaver of your own life, or are you the fly trapped on someone else's web? Are your heartstrings too sensitive and keeping you from experiencing love? If the spider's web gets damaged, she just builds another one. Is it time for you to reweave your fate and destiny?

Throat

As mentioned above, in some cultures, the spider was the teacher of written language, which means writing is or can be an excellent form of communication for you. Since spiders have no ears and feel sounds rather than hearing them, it is possible that you feel sound in a way that can make you super sensitive. If you are someone that has sound sensitivity, it may be difficult for you to go out in public. If noises get too overwhelming for you, try to seek out quiet places or try wearing sound-canceling headphones whenever you can. Another possible interpretation of the spider in this chakra says that you are someone that can literally *feel* if someone is telling the truth or not. If this is the case for you, trust this instinct; it is a useful one to have.

Third Eye

Even though spiders have eight eyes, their eyesight is not that great. They depend more on feeling than on what they can see. As mentioned earlier, the hair that covers a spider's legs is incredibly sensitive to even minute changes in vibration. This says your psychic sight is often more accurate than your actual eyesight, so you should trust it. A spider hangs from above, seeing the whole picture, so this aspect speaks to the ability to see from a different perspective or point of view. The fact that the spider's web is transparent means you see *through* a situation instead of seeing only walls. Hanging from your web is also an excellent opportunity to gain introspection about your own life situation. As suggested in the bat section, you may want to try inversion meditation.

Crown

The spider is the weaver of fate in many cultures and symbolizes all things related to balance: life and death, male and female, light and dark, and more. The spider says you are aware of this balance and connect with your divine self while still being grounded.

SQUIRREL

Currently, more than two hundred species of squirrel can be found worldwide, except in Australia and Antarctica. Squirrels can be broken down into three groups: tree, ground, and flying. Tree squirrels live in woodlands and forests, ground squirrels live in areas that include grasslands and tundra, and flying squirrels live in the woods. Even within their group, different species will compete for territory, sometimes viciously, but the general nature of squirrels is playful, loving, and protective. They are also incredibly intelligent and resourceful, as anyone who has tried to keep them out of a bird feeder knows. They can solve any puzzle or obstacle that keeps them from what they want. They are also the epitome of preparedness, teaching the lesson to always be ready for a rainy day.

Key Attributes

Playfulness, resourcefulness, planning for the future, trust, achieving one's goals through determination and hard work, socialization, chatty conversation, cleverness, and a reminder to have fun.

Chakra Interpretations

Root

Most people think squirrels only eat nuts and what they can steal from a bird feeder, but this is not the case. Squirrels are omnivores, meaning they eat both plants and meat. Squirrels will sometimes pretend to bury food to throw off potential thieves. They also hide nuts in lots of different locations and no one is entirely sure if they can remember all of them. Nuts that get left behind contribute to reforestation. You may have a habit of "squirreling away" food in various parts of your house, office, or car. Another possibility for the squirrel in this chakra is that you are very good with investments. You don't put all your money in one place but have mastered the art of diversifying. One more possibility is a warning that you may be accumulating way too much stuff and becoming a pack rat. Is it time to clear out your nest?

Sacral

Squirrels will run in unpredictable routes to confuse possible predators. People may have a hard time keeping up with you, which might be intentional on your part to keep them guessing and your way of staying ahead of your game. It is also possible that your energy has become scattered and you need to focus or nothing will get done. If this is the case, slow down, quiet your mind, and remember to breathe. Another aspect of squirrel is that they learn best when working with their hands. Building something practical or just creating something beautiful for the sheer joy of creating can bring you a lot of satisfaction.

Solar Plexus

Squirrel is the epitome of hard work and preparation because it spends all its waking hours toiling. If this sounds like you, while your intentions are honorable, it might be that you are neglecting not only the people closest to you but yourself as well. The bills will probably still get paid, and food will be on the table even if you take a night off now and then to be with those you love. They are the reason you work so hard, and you need to remember that. Another possible interpretation has to do with one particular species, the flying squirrel. If you have been resisting making changes in your life, this little guy is telling you to take a leap of faith and soar. Another characteristic of the squirrel is that it is one of the few wild animals that will eat out of a human's hand. Squirrel energy may be telling you that it is okay to accept a gift or a handout. The person doing the giving may not have an agenda other than to help you.

Heart

A squirrel's heart beats very fast. From a practical standpoint, this could mean you are prone to high blood pressure. Meditative practices can help, but don't shy away from medication if it is necessary. The territorial and chaotic nature of squirrel could be a reminder that it is time to calm down. If you want to find peace in your heart, you must first find harmony and balance in your life. Slow down and take a breath. Squirrels can be very trusting, but when they are frightened or sense danger, they will stop and remain motionless. The squirrel could be asking what the status of your heart is: open and trusting or frozen with fear? If it is fearful, identify the source of your anxiety and get away from it to safety. If it is open and trusting, then that is a beautiful thing.

Throat

Squirrels are very vocal in both work and play, and their nonstop chatter can create a sense of confusion. It might be that you feel like you need to talk louder than other people to get your point across. It very well could be that you thrive in situations like this, but if not, try to calm the chaos and seek silence. Another way squirrels communicate is with their tails. It is possible that your body language is easy to read; just make sure the signals you are projecting are the ones you want it to send.

Third Eye

Squirrels' eyes can see a significant amount of their surroundings without their bodies or heads needing to move. This says that you are aware of everything going on around you, while others think you aren't even paying attention. At the same time, it may be time to stop the inner chatter of your mind so you *can* pay attention.

Crown

Many species of squirrel spend most of their time in trees, and while they do not hibernate, they do sleep a lot, especially during cold weather. You might be the kind of person who only crawls out from under the covers because you must. Your best way to recharge is by slowing down and spending time in the dream world. If this sounds like you, you know yourself well enough to know that you need to shut off the outside world and bury yourself in your nest. Only when you do this can you hear the messages not only from your higher self but also from Spirit and the universe.

STAG

Myths surrounding the stag have existed throughout time. When used in a heraldry crest, a stag or stag's antlers represented peace and harmony, strength and fortitude, and one who would not fight unless provoked. In many cultures, the stag represents masculinity and sexuality. Even in nature, a stag's antlers are symbolic of their dominance within the ranks of other stags, and the bigger the rack the more virile they are thought to be.

Key Attributes

Pride, courage, protection, guardianship, beauty, dignity and majesty, athleticism, authority, connection to the seasons and renewal, and achieving one's goals through determination and perseverance.

Chakra Interpretations

Root

A stag can adapt to living pretty much anywhere. It is thought by some researchers that young stags stay on the move until they find a spot that they like but the older a stag becomes the less likely he is to want to move to a new territory. Most of us move around a few times when we are younger, but once we finally settle, the thought of needing to move is no longer appealing. If stag speaks to you in this chakra, you have most likely found the home you want to stay in for the long term. Another aspect of the stag in this chakra comes from the fact that he will fight vigorously with his antlers, sometimes even to the death, to show dominance and claim territory. You take great pride in protecting what you consider yours and are willing to fight to keep it, be it your home, your family, or even projects at work. It could also be that you work in the field of wildlife protection or conservation.

Sacral

Stag energy is very connected to the earth. You have your feet planted firmly on the ground, and you carry yourself with pride. One not-so-flattering aspect of a stag in this chakra could be saying that sex is just a release for you and intimacy doesn't enter the equation. As long as your partner understands and agrees to it, then no one will get hurt. Another aspect of stag speaks to the power of renewal. Just as the stag grows a new set of antlers every year, if challenges in your life have left you depleted, know that you can regrow your natural crown of power as well. Yet another aspect speaks to its athleticism. A stag can run as fast as 35 miles an hour, albeit for short distances, and is a powerful swimmer. One possible meaning for you is that you are passionate about one or even both of these activities. They could be a good way for you to release tension.

Solar Plexus

Regardless of the species, the stag projects unquestionable majesty. This means that you carry yourself with a sense of pride, dignity, and leadership that few doubt. You do this not from a place of ego, but from knowing that it is your role to be a guardian and a protector. As mentioned earlier, a stag in heraldry represented someone who would not fight unless provoked. You will try several means of conflict resolution before resorting to anything drastic, but if all other options fail, you will do whatever is necessary to defend not only yourself but those you love. Another aspect speaks to the fact that stag grows a new set of antlers each year. It is possible that your leadership roles have changed over time, but each time it has, you filled the new role with dignity.

Heart

Stags are primarily solitary creatures. It could be that you are on your own by personal choice, but if it is due to past hurts, stag in this chakra is a reminder that just like the planet, the human heart goes through seasons. We all experience periods when we feel overwhelmed by emotion, but those storms do eventually pass. Even after the coldest winter, new life sprouts and spring returns, so trust in your own renewal. The stag inspires fantasy, romance, and imagination. Not so flattering, but it might be that you are more attached to the *dream* of love and are not willing to put in the effort it takes for a relationship to work long-term.

Throat

A stag's vocalizations change depending on mood and intent, but if there is no cause for alarm or need to communicate, he stays quiet. Most likely, you are a person of few words, preferring to speak only when necessary, and when you do, there is always a good reason. If a stag feels lonely he will call out for companionship. Maybe you need a guys' night now and then, even if you don't identify as one. A stag will make a series of rage grunts if a female refuses him. You might be prone to very vocal temper tantrums if you don't get your way. Go ahead and stomp your feet and grunt a bit, but then get over it and move on.

Third Eye

Because his eyes are on the sides of his head, a stag sees roughly 310 degrees; however, he can't focus on one location with both eyes at the same time, so he has poor depth perception. It could be that you are able to see the big picture of a situation but miss the details. Spiritually, the stag brings the gifts of prophecy and second sight. This combination of aspects says your mind's eye is naturally sensitive, and you see a vast range—perhaps you are even adept at distance viewing.

Crown

A stag has an innate majesty and dignity that is without question, and those with stag energy are not only natural leaders but guardians as well. It could be that you feel called to be a teacher to those on a spiritual path that worships and honors nature. Your inborn bond to the wild places will help guide seekers so they learn how to develop their own direct connection without falling down a hypothetical rabbit hole. At the same time, this is a reminder to not lose your own connection. If you have been feeling ungrounded and a little lost, maybe it is time for a trip to the woods so you can plug back in to your source and recharge.

SWAN

Swans are one of those creatures whose very image brings up thoughts of love, beauty, and grace. Considered by some to be one of the most ancient of power animals, swans have been the inspiration of bards, musicians, and even the ballet for ages. Like in the story of "The Ugly Duckling," swans represent transformation and the ability to find your inner beauty and to see the hidden beauty of others. Like crows and many other birds, swans will remember humans who have been nice to them and as well as those who have not. While trumpeter and tundra swans are native to North America, mute swans are not; they were imports from Europe during the mid-1800s to ornament large estates, city parks, and zoos. Fugitives from these captive immigrants formed breeding populations and now live in the Northeast, mid-Atlantic, Great Lakes, and Pacific Northwest.

Key Attributes

Inner grace and beauty, balance, self-esteem, intuitive ability, personal commitment, love, music, poetry, transformation, and letting go of childhood pain.

Chakra Interpretations

Root

Swans live in different habitats depending on the species, but what they all have in common is water. Living near water or spending time on the water is essential to you. Most likely, your preferred home life consists of two loving parents raising children together in a supportive environment. Another aspect of the swan speaks of their tendency to be grumpy and honk and chase away anyone who comes too close to their territory. You are very protective of your home and family, and you might be the person on your street who yells at the neighborhood children or dogs to stay off your lawn.

Sacral

If you had a difficult childhood or have a negative self-image, swan energy is telling you to let go of past pain and acknowledge all that you have overcome. Beauty comes from your inner strength, and those difficult times are long past. It is also a reminder that we all go through transformations throughout our lives, and we should strive to accept those changes with dignity. It might be that you are leaving your college years and entering the business world, which requires a different wardrobe. You might be entering your crone years (even if you are not a woman) and leaving your youth behind. Regardless of your transformation stage, the important thing is to do it with grace and style!

Solar Plexus

Even though it is one of the largest aquatic birds, the graceful swan barely leaves a wake and speaks to your ability to carry yourself with poise. Even if you are physically larger than others around you, no matter where you go, you project elegance. Another aspect of swans is that, though beautiful and graceful, they can be a little ill-tempered. They hiss and attack anything or anyone that enters their territory or comes near their eggs or babies. You might be the prettiest or most handsome person in the room, and people may have a perception of you because of that external physical appearance, but don't let them forget that you are perfectly capable of defending yourself and those you love. At the same time, don't expect an outer beauty to be your only virtue. You still need to treat people with the respect you desire for yourself.

Heart

Swans are monogamous and will stay with one partner for many years, sometimes mating for life. They are very protective and affectionate with each other. When they are courting, they will bow toward each other and curve their necks to form the classic image of a heart. When you are in a relationship, most likely you are very protective of your partner and never tire from romantic expressions of love, be it a candlelight dinner, a walk on the beach, or a spontaneous slow dance in the kitchen. Showing your partner love and affection feeds your soul and keeps your love alive. If you are not in a relationship, this love could be for children, companion animals, or even work or a creative project. The key message here is whomever or whatever you give your heart to, they will have it completely.

Throat

A swan's long neck is beautiful and symbolic of grace and beauty. Swan in this chakra says you have no problem speaking your mind or speaking up for someone or something dear to you. When you communicate, you do so with eloquence and style. The term *swan song* comes from the mistaken belief that a mute swan only sings just before dying as a final act of beauty. Today it has come to mean a last creative expression or final performance. If you connect with swan in this chakra, ask yourself if it is time for you to give your swan song performance and move on to something new.

Third Eye

Just like how they leave virtually no wake while swimming, swan energy says you can enter the land of the unconscious without leaving a wake as well. When you approach the realm of Spirit, you do so from a place of honor and beauty. If this has been a challenge for you, just as the ugly duckling was able to transform its physical self, the swan is telling you that you can transform your intuitive self as well.

Crown

Living a life of grace doesn't mean just on the physical plane, it also means showing grace with your spiritual existence as well. Some believe that we are humans searching for a spiritual experience. Others believe we are spirits learning how to have a human experience, and still others think it is a combination of the two, that we shouldn't think of them as separate. Regardless of which concept is real, the challenge is to maintain grace on the journey. The swan is letting you know that your connection with Spirit is divine, and by surrendering to that beauty, you will find peace and tranquility.

TURKEY

The big round birds that most people picture when they think of turkeys are descended from domestic birds that were originally from Mexico and were symbols of gratitude and abundance long before the American Thanksgiving holiday. Known as *Give-Away Eagle* in some Native American cultures and *Peace Eagle* in others, the turkey speaks to the willingness to share or give up just about everything so that others do not go without. They remind us to be grateful for the bounty in our lives and never to take abundance for granted. They also remind us that it is vital to maintain a harmonious relationship with the land and environment.

Key Attributes

Abundance, fertility, gratitude, generosity, sacrifice, and pride.

Chakra Interpretations

Root

Wild turkeys live in forested areas interspersed with clearings. They tend to stay in mostly single-sex flocks, with poults staying with their mothers, that range in size from five to fifty individuals in an area that can be over a thousand acres, and they learn and remember exact details of every inch. You may be most comfortable living in a wooded setting or at the very least in a place where you are rarely alone. For you to feel safe, this may not need to be in the woods, but it does need to be somewhere you can blend in to your environment. It is possible that you don't live in a traditional family structure but with friends or relatives of your same gender. The Give-Away Eagle aspect says you are the kind of person who takes nothing for granted, that you are grateful for all that you have and are willing to share even if you have very little yourself.

Sacral

Turkey shows that what brings you pleasure is understanding the connection of your existence to your natural and social environment and that you feel a personal responsibility to it. You might be an avid environmentalist and the earth and her creatures are your passion. It could be that you work in the environmental sciences professionally or are the one who starts a recycling plan in your neighborhood, school, or workplace. Another possible passion for you is gifting. If you see or know of someone in need, you will go out of your way to help them.

Solar Plexus

Despite their size, turkeys can run and fly very fast, albeit for short distances. One interpretation of this is to not let other people assume you aren't capable of being quick on your feet. Female turkeys have brown feathers that help them blend into their environment, and it is usually only the rustling of leaves that gives their presence away. Does your feminine aspect only feel safe and happy when you are invisible? An aspect of the male turkey speaks to his tendency to show off. Like peacocks, male turkeys will puff up their bodies and spread their elaborate feathers to attract a mate. It doesn't matter if you are competing for love or a job—make sure you aren't puffing yourself up to be bigger or more important than you are so the lie doesn't come back to haunt you later. On the other side of this, it might be time for you to show off a little so people take notice of you.

Heart

Turkeys are very social, and the emotional ties they create are long-lasting. It is likely that you have a close relationship with a group of friends that you have known for a very long time. There are several additional possibilities at play here. Most likely, you prefer the company of your same gender and aren't drawn to monogamous relationships. If you identify with mostly the male aspect of yourself, you probably don't feel any draw toward parental duties, but if you identify with your feminine side, you are a natural mother and prefer the company of other women. As mentioned, turkey energy is giving, and it undoubtedly brings your heart great satisfaction to be providing for others.

Throat

The turkey has an area of bare skin covering its throat and head called a *wattle* that changes color depending on the turkey's mood. This wattle turns vivid red during courtship or if the turkey is angry, but if the bird is calm it remains blue or gray. This says your emotions color how you communicate, allowing others to read you easily. In addition to their classic gobble, turkeys exhibit over twenty distinct vocalizations, which can be heard at least a mile away. This aspect of the turkey says you can benefit others by speaking up for them, even if it is via long-distance communication.

Third Eye

Turkeys have excellent vision, seeing three times more clearly than 20/20, and can detect motion from many yards away. The position of their eyes gives the turkey a visual field of nearly 270 degrees; add to this its ability to rotate its neck and that visual range increases to nearly 360 degrees. The only downside is that they lack binocular vision, so they don't have much in the way of depth perception. There probably isn't very much that misses your attention or awareness, but a downside might be that you don't look very deeply at something—you only see what is on the surface. Another aspect of turkeys is that they have been known to show agitation before inclement weather. It may be that you are prone to headaches or feel slightly dizzy when the barometric pressure changes or you might experience body aches that let you know that it is going to rain.

Crown

Turkeys stay close to the ground during the day to forage but rest high up in trees away from predators at night for safety. It may be difficult for you to relax enough to sleep due to some unspoken or invisible fear or stress. If this is the case, try doing a grounding meditation before bed or even drinking an herbal relaxation tea. Turkey also speaks to you of the power of dream time; use your dreams to draw abundance to you and to help you connect with the natural world from other realms.

TURTLE

The turtle is one of the world's oldest living creatures. No matter your belief system, this fact alone shows that turtle represents longevity and can help you with your connection to time. In many cultures, the turtle is a symbol for Mother Earth, and in some First Nations stories, North America was called Turtle Island. *Turtle* is the blanket term for all turtles, tortoises, and terrapins, though many people interchange the terms *tortoise* and *turtle*. While both are reptiles and members of the order Testudines, there are distinct differences. Tortoises are land dwellers and plant eaters, and their shells are round and domed. Turtles can live on land or water, most are omnivores, and their shells are more streamlined. One similarity is that both love to bask in the sun.

Key Attributes

A reminder to honor the planet, fertility, protection, patience, moving at one's own pace, being grounded, longevity, achieving goals with determination and endurance, and stability.

Chakra Interpretations

Root

Turtles are long-lived, solitary creatures that move at their own pace. It is very possible that longevity runs in your family. Turtles are connected to both earth and water, and they carry their home on their back. You probably have very few requirements when it comes to where you choose to live as long as the environment provides your basic needs. You may also be the kind of person who lives a minimalist lifestyle, keeping only those personal belongings that can be quickly packed and easily transported. Your motivation could be due to some traumatic event in your life history, or it could merely be a personal choice. Either way, being unencumbered by *stuff* helps you keep a sense of freedom, so you never have to rely on anyone else when you are ready to move on.

Sacral

Turtle in this chakra says that you may have developed an outer shell around your sexuality or your life's passions. Just like we humans can't feel our hair or fingernails but we can tell when they are touched, a turtle senses when its shell contacts something. If you have experienced some form of trauma or even a string of life events that have left you feeling numb, it can be healing to climb into the turtle's shell for a while. Just be sure it does not become your permanent state of being.

Solar Plexus

As mentioned earlier, turtles move at their own speed. You are the kind of person who can't be rushed. Some may perceive you as lazy or slow, but that is not always the case. It may be that you prefer to take your time before committing to any endeavor. It may also be that you like to thoroughly investigate a situation before acting. Then again, you may be the kind of person who takes forever to get ready to go anywhere, whose work is always late, or whose friends and family must give them a much earlier meeting time for them to show up at a particular place on schedule. Only by being honest with yourself can you decide which of these matches you. A turtle may be slow, but its smallest actions and behaviors can speak volumes. If you tend to make decisions too quickly, turtle energy can teach you how to slow down and think before you act.

Heart

A turtle's shell has blood vessels and feels physical touch. If damaged, their shell will bleed and the turtle will feel pain. Most turtles, even pet turtles, don't like to be touched. The turtle in this chakra could mean that because of life experiences you have closed your heart for fear of being hurt. Like a turtle living in a cold climate, have you gone into hibernation? Opening your heart again is not something you need to rush. Give yourself time to heal, and do it at your own pace, not because of outside pressure. At the same time remember that to truly live, eventually you have to emerge from your shell and let warmth seep back in.

Throat

Some species of turtle can close into their shell completely when startled. They have very few vocalizations, and when they do make sound, it is usually a hiss of fear. The turtle in this chakra could mean that it is hard for you to speak or perform in front of people. If this is the case, try practicing in a safe space in front of a mirror or with people who will encourage you. Another possibility could be that you have trouble speaking up for yourself, and when you do, it comes across as defensive. Remember that not everyone is out to get you. Some people might be approaching you out of curiosity and could be allies in disguise.

Third Eye

Of the senses that turtles possess, eyesight is their most reliable, which could mean that this chakra is one of your strongest. You not only see reality, but you also see through the filters that watery emotions can cause. Turtles do not have external ears; they pick up the vibrations that sounds make rather than hearing the way that humans do. The turtle in this chakra could mean you are highly sensitive to even the slightest energetic vibrations. Don't let a hard shell of nonbelief limit you from acknowledging what you are seeing and sensing is real.

Crown

The turtle rose sometime during the late Triassic period and has existed practically unchanged to the present day, connecting them and you to concepts of time on this earthly plane. The turtle in this chakra is your gateway to tapping into ancient earth histories and wisdom. It is also a reminder that for you to continue your evolution, you need to slow down, take a breath, and approach Spirit from a place of peace. Take a clue from turtles that hibernate and consider adding deep trance work to your practice so you can make these connections.

WHALE

Similar to how the wolf's howl is an iconic sound of the wilderness and night, the song of whales is iconic of the sea, and both sounds call to something deep and primordial in our souls. Considered to be some of the most complex nonhuman communication, the song of whales can be heard for many miles. Both male and female whales are capable of vocalization, but only male humpbacks produce the long, intricate melodies most of us are most familiar with. Unlike humans, whose breathing is automatic, whales are voluntary breathers, meaning they think about every breath they take. Some cultures believe that the whale is the keeper of the world's ancient memories. Whale energy helps you understand the history of life on earth and your most rooted connection to the universe.

Key Attributes

Keeper of the earth's records, honoring the sacred, the power of song, the beauty of movement, grace, intelligence, and telepathic ability.

Chakra Interpretations

Root

While able to live alone, whales prefer to live in communities, from groups as small as a few members to large pods that cross many generations. Whales have a family structure that they are very devoted to. They communicate with each other, teach their young, and even mourn the loss of a member. Your family is what gives you a strong foundation in life. One whale species, the killer whale, also known as the orca, is organized in matriarchal groups in which the female is dominant. If you connect with this whale, you might come from a family with very strong females and maybe even a matriarch that runs everyone's lives. One more aspect of the whale in this chakra comes from the whale as record keeper and is speaking to you from your past and asking you to understand where you come from. If you haven't already, you might consider getting a DNA test done so you know what your ancestral history is.

Sacral

Whales have a social hierarchy, play games together, teach each other survival strategies, and hunt in cohesive, well-organized groups. Social contact and interaction are critical to nearly all whale species, and this speaks to your need for close connections as well, if not from your family of origin, then from your family of choice. One of the classic images of the whale is that of breaching. No one knows why whales breach; it could be a mating display, it could be some practical reason we aren't aware of, or it could be for the fun of it. Whatever the reason, whale is telling you to find your joy and leap into it.

Solar Plexus

It is possible that you have a larger-than-life personality, and you use it with gentleness and intelligence for the benefit of not only yourself but also of those around you. You are self-aware and comfortable in your skin. If you identify with an orca matriarch, it could be that you have a very strong personality, and be it at home or at work, you dominate. It is a role you feel you earned by life experience. However, if you find that people tend to be afraid of you and you don't want them to be, maybe taking a clue from a gentler whale would benefit not only you but those under your charge. One more aspect speaks to the whale's fundamental need to breathe. If a situation is causing you to feel like you are drowning, it may be time to find a place of calm so you can catch your breath and float your way to the surface and safety.

Heart

The heart of a whale is typically the size of a small car, and the heartbeat of the blue whale can be detected as far as two miles away. Whale in this chakra says your heart is as big as the ocean is deep, and you are willing to share anything and everything you have. If someone you care for is buried in problems or sorrow, you are often the one to try to nudge them gently toward the surface to safety and air. The whale can dive to great depths, which might be a suggestion for you to dive into the depths of your own emotions to find the song in your heart. This song can carry long distances and will keep you connected with those you love.

Throat

Different species of whale have different vocalizations, but all of them use sound to communicate and socialize with each other. Just like humans, whose accents can change depending on where they live, differing vocal dialects have been found to exist between different pods within the same whale population. On a similar note, researchers have discovered that males of one group will sing the same song together, while whales in another region or hemisphere will sing a completely different song, but also in unison. It could be that you have a knack for picking up different dialects or that you work in a language-oriented field. You may even be multilingual. Another interpretation is that you have a love of singing, particularly if it is with a group.

Third Eye

When whales sleep, not only do they stay at the top of the water with their blowhole above the surface, but only half their brain sleeps while the other half stays awake. It could be that you are skilled at being in deep meditation while staying partially alert. It could even mean that you are proficient at lucid dreaming. Toothed whales navigate the ocean by using echolocation. This aspect could say that you are clairaudient or that you should try using sound to open this chakra. Try listening to whale song in meditation or for going to sleep.

Crown

As mentioned earlier, whales breathe from the crown and have to think about every breath they take. Whale energy acknowledges that you already have a profound cosmic consciousness; you just need to trust it and remember to breathe. Whale is the ancient record keeper and may help you connect with your own Akashic story. Try visualizing breathing from this chakra, and you might just be able to tap into those records.

WOLF

The wolf has played the lead role in countless fairy tales and myths for ages. Once thought of as a threat, scientists now understand the beneficial cascade effect wolves play in restoring and revitalizing an ecosystem, giving them the classification as a keystone species. Their presence has a series of direct and indirect effects on the diversity and abundance of both plant and animal life. Recent studies have concluded that, similar to how humans and whales around the world "speak" in different dialects, wolves do too, and each dialect is unique to that region. Additionally, an individual wolf's howl is unique, much like a fingerprint.

Key Attributes

Strength of family ties, inner knowing, being in harmony with nature, honoring the sacred, pride and dignity, ability to love a partner for life, intelligence, and defending one's boundaries.

Chakra Interpretations

Root

Wolves are highly intelligent, social creatures who are very caring, playful, and deeply devoted to family. Wolves educate their young, care for their injured, and live in family groups, and a mated pair of wolves typically mates for life. Adult family members help care for the pups, even babysitting while others hunt, and members will even sacrifice themselves to protect the family unit. The wolf shows that family and community are very important to you. Whether it is your family of origin or your family of choice, being a member of a pack is essential to your survival and what makes you feel safe. As far as partnerships go, if you have already found your life mate, then you are one of the lucky ones. If not, do not settle for less than your equal.

Sacral

A person who is extremely independent is often called a *lone wolf.* Both male and female wolves may go through periods of being alone, but a wolf on its own is a wolf that wants to be with other wolves. While a wolf maintains its identity, its very nature tells it that it needs to belong to a pack. It knows it succeeds by cooperating and struggles for survival when alone. You are probably happiest and can be at your best when you are part of a pack; it gives you a level of safety and freedom to be your most authentic self.

Solar Plexus

It was once thought that wolves lived in structured, unchanging hierarchies with an alpha pair in the lead. However, there have been some current studies that show that a wolf pack's structure and relationships go through a natural fluctuation that can change over time and even over the seasons. There is still a lead or alpha pair, but researchers now describe packs more in terms of family units. You understand that there is balance and discipline in respecting the pecking order and your role in it, be it as the alpha or as support, and that your role may change from time to time. Another interpretation of the wolf in this chakra relates to a wolf's endurance. A wolf can't move very fast, but it will follow its prey until the prey tires out, all day and night if need be. This speaks to your ability to go the distance. Whatever task you undertake, you will see it through to completion. You may be one known for pulling an all-nighter to get the job done.

Heart

Touch being the sense of this chakra, it will come as no surprise that wolves use touch to communicate their feelings. Wolves form lifelong bonds, will play together well into their old age, and grieve at the loss of a member of the pack. It is possible that you have a group of friends that you have known for most of your life, and you continue to enjoy each other's company. It could also mean that you have strong ties to your family, not just siblings, but aunts, uncles, and cousins as well.

Where a life mate is concerned, if you haven't already found one, your preference would be to find one partner and to stay with them for life.

Throat

Primal and penetrating, the howl of the wolf is one of the most iconic symbols of night, but wolves use more than just their howl to communicate with each other. Howls seem to be about togetherness, whether the wolves are gathering for a hunt, mourning a lost pack mate, or announcing territorial or mating intentions. The wolf is telling you that silence is lonely and only by howling will you find your pack. The sense connected with this chakra is hearing. After smell, hearing is the wolf's strongest sense; it can hear as far as six miles in a wooded area and up to ten miles in an open area. Wolf energy acknowledges that you are always willing to listen to a friend or family member and might even be able to hear their call in your mind, even from a long distance away.

Third Eye

A wolf's eyes are optimized to detect motion, and they have excellent peripheral and night vision. The wolf is telling you to tap into your wolf vision, your inner knowing and intuition. Depending on the level of light pollution where you live, spend time under the night sky starring at the moon and stars. Given that the wolf is at its best in a pack, if you work with a spiritual group or have a life mate, try connecting with them psychically to build a dream lodge where you can practice meeting up on the astral plane.

Crown

In some cultures, the wolf guards the doors that allow entrance to the celestial realms, and in others, wolves are considered teachers and pathfinders. As suggested above, try to spend time outside under the night sky or visualizing the moon while meditating. Call on wolf energy to help you unlock the doors to your inner knowing; you might be surprised by the path that opens to you.

WREN

Wrens are a perfect example of good things coming in small packages. A wren may be hard to spot because of its tiny size and brown coloring, but it has a repertoire of songs so vast and loud that once you hear it, it's hard to imagine so much sound coming out of such a tiny creature. Its voice is a sign of spring to many. This little bird is considered the Druid bird in the British Isles, the king of all birds by the Celts, and Lady of Souls hen in Scotland. An interesting fact about wrens is that they have been known to use spider egg sacs in their nest building, and it is believed that once the eggs hatch, the baby spiders will eat any parasites that might be in the nest, keeping the chicks healthier.

Key Attributes

Friendliness, lightheartedness, love of music and poetry, resourcefulness, and boldness despite size.

Chakra Interpretations

Root

The wren is a resourceful little bird, able to make a nest pretty much anywhere. A male wren seeks out a location and starts the nest-building process, often building as many as twelve different nesting sites before the female decides which one they will use. It is possible that if you lean toward the male aspect of the wren, you will do whatever it takes to please your partner, even if that means doing a similar task over and over again until she is happy. If you resonate with the female aspect of wren, you probably let your partner do all the preliminary work and then come in to put on the finishing touches. This partnership can be a love relationship, a creative collaboration, or even a work situation.

Sacral

Some wrens can be found year-round in the southern half of the Americas, but those that live in the United States and the northern part of Central America are migratory, residing in the north during spring and summer and flying south for the winter. Like a wren, for you to be happy, you need to be warm. You might even be a snowbird, heading south in the winter months to escape the cold, or at the very least vacationing somewhere warm. One particular species, the Carolina wren, is monogamous and both partners work together to construct nests. If you (and your partner or spouse) connect with this wren, it could be that you run a business together or at the very least like to do as much together as possible.

Solar Plexus

A fierce competitor for nest holes, the wren will sometimes evict other wrens and even much larger birds to get the home it wants. Wren energy shows that you have a great deal of confidence, and once you decide what you want, you are willing to work hard and if necessary fight to get it. Everyone who knows you knows that you are highly competitive, even aggressively so. If there is something that you have set your mind to, there is no limit to the action you will take, no matter whom you hurt the process. If this aspect rings true to you, you might want to try being a little kinder so karma doesn't come along to bite you. Unlike most birds that have colorful plumage, making them easy to spot, both male and female wrens blend into the surrounding environment. This can be an excellent form of protection, but if you feel like you are disappearing into the scenery; it may be time to learn how to be a little flashy if you want to stand out from the crowd.

Heart

Male house wrens will sometimes pair with two females at the same time or mate with one at the start of the season and then mate with a second, or even third, female as the season passes. If this type of wren speaks to you, most likely you are happiest in a polyamorous relationship. If that is the case, just make sure everyone agrees to that arrangement. However, as mentioned, Carolina wrens are monogamous and form a bond that lasts for life. This bonded pair not only builds their nest together, but they do everything together, including raising their young. If this is the wren that speaks to you, then most likely you are not happy in a relationship unless it is a monogamous relationship of equals, and once you find it, you are willing to stay for life.

Throat

With most wren species, such as the Carolina wren, only the male sings, but with the house wren, both males and females sing. To some, the song of the wren is a sure sign that the long winter is over. You can hear their effervescent song from sunrise to sunset. If you connect with wren in this chakra, your voice can brighten any room. One way to put this energy to good use is to visit places like nursing homes or hospitals. It doesn't matter if you are singing by yourself, with a partner, or with a group. Use your voice to spread joy.

Third Eye

Even though they are territorial, wrens are shy birds and prefer someplace quiet to build their nests. Some like a place they can crawl into, but others will build a nest in a hanging porch plant, as long as it is in an out-of-the-way area with little disturbance. For you to be able to be open to this chakra, you need to find a quiet place where you won't be disturbed. It could be that your favorite place is to crawl into a tent, but another option for you would be to relax in a hammock. Either place would help you shut off the outside world so you can tap into any intuitive messages that are trying to come through.

Crown

Wren being a bird mostly of spring represents a time of regeneration and rebirth. Wren energy may be asking if you have grown tired of the same meditations. Is it time to try a new practice, something that will breathe life back into your connection with your higher self? Maybe it is time to add singing to your spiritual practice. No matter your religious beliefs, song can bring you closer to your concept of Spirit.

CONNECTIONS

What follows is a list of possible connections between you and certain animals. If there is something about yourself of which you are already aware, the list may help you find animals you may already have a connection with but hadn't considered. The same can be said for something you would like to work on about yourself. The list is by no means all-inclusive, but it may help you find some surprises.

Abundance

Buffalo	Frog
Rabbit	Turkey

Achieving Goals

Ant	Armadillo
Badger	Beaver
Bee	Crow
Eagle	Hawk
Heron	Moose
Octopus	Otter
Raven	Salmon
Squirrel	Stag
Turtle	

Adaptability

Coyote
Horse
Hummingbird
Mouse
Octopus
Owl
Porcupine
Raccoon
Raven
Skunk
Spider
Stag
Wren

Aging or Maturity (Changes Related to)

Bee
Dragonfly
Hummingbird
Salmon
Stag
Swan
Whale

Akashic or Earth Records

Frog
Hawk
Owl
Salmon
Turtle
Whale

Ancestral Knowledge

Badger
Bear
Mouse
Owl
Salmon
Whale

Anger/Temper

Badger
Bear
Hummingbird
Seal
Skunk
Stag

Asking for or Providing Help

Dog
Dolphin
Horse
Turkey
Whale

Authority

Badger
Bear
Eagle
Hawk
Mountain Lion
Owl
Stag

Blessings from, Messages from, or Connection to Spirit

Crow
Deer
Dove
Eagle
Grouse
Hawk
Horse
Owl
Raven
Salmon
Snake
Spider
Stag
Swan

Boundaries (Personal)

Armadillo
Badger
Bear
Mountain Lion
Owl
Porcupine
Skunk
Squirrel
Stag
Swan
Wolf

Camouflage

Coyote
Deer
Fox
Frog
Grouse
Lizard
Moose
Mouse
Octopus
Owl
Rabbit
Raccoon
Turtle

Childlike Nature

Armadillo Coyote
Otter Porcupine
Raccoon

Cleverness

Cat Coyote
Fox Mouse
Opossum Otter
Raccoon Squirrel

Collaboration (Satisfaction from)

Ant Beaver
Bee Dolphin
Horse Otter
Whale Wolf

Communication

Ant Bee
Coyote Crow
Dolphin Fox
Mouse Octopus
Owl Raven
Seal Spider
Squirrel Whale
Wolf

Community

Ant Bat
Beaver Bee
Crow Dog
Dolphin Horse
Otter Rabbit
Raven Turkey
Whale Wolf

Competitive Nature

Buffalo (male)
Squirrel
Turkey (male)
Wren

Confidence

Badger
Bear
Cat
Crow
Dog
Eagle
Hawk
Heron
Horse
Lizard
Mountain Lion
Owl
Raven
Salmon
Stag
Wren

Courage, Bravery, or Fearlessness

Badger
Bear
Buffalo
Cat
Crow
Deer
Eagle
Fox
Hawk
Horse
Moose
Mountain Lion
Owl
Raven
Salmon
Skunk
Stag
Wolf

Creativity or Making or Building Things

Beaver
Butterfly
Crow
Mouse
Opossum
Otter
Raccoon
Raven
Spider
Squirrel
Wren

Curiosity or Exploring the Unknown

Bat	Cat
Dragonfly	Fox
Hawk	Lizard
Mouse	Otter
Owl	Porcupine
Raccoon	Raven
Seal	Spider

Dance

Bee	Grouse
Hawk	Porcupine

Defensiveness

Armadillo	Badger
Dog	Moose
Octopus	Opossum
Porcupine	Skunk
Stag	

Determination or Perseverance

Ant	Armadillo
Badger	Bee
Crow	Eagle
Frog	Hawk
Heron	Octopus
Otter	Mouse
Raven	Salmon
Spider	Squirrel
Stag	Turtle

Dignity or Pride

Cat
Deer
Eagle
Hawk
Heron
Horse
Mountain Lion
Owl
Raven
Stag
Swan
Turkey
Wolf

Dreaming

Bear
Beaver
Cat
Crow
Dolphin
Dove
Dragonfly
Horse
Lizard
Owl
Salmon
Seal
Stag
Turtle
Whale

Empathy

Ant
Coyote
Crow
Dog
Dove
Frog
Horse
Otter
Raven
Swan
Whale
Wolf

Facing Fear

Armadillo
Bat
Deer
Mouse
Octopus
Opossum
Porcupine
Rabbit
Raven
Skunk
Snake
Squirrel
Turtle

Family or Social Ties

Bat
Beaver
Bee
Coyote
Crow
Dog
Dolphin
Dove
Eagle
Fox
Horse
Otter
Rabbit
Raven
Seal
Squirrel
Turkey
Whale
Wolf

Femininity

Deer
Dove
Fox
Frog
Mountain Lion
Otter
Spider

Fertility

Bee
Frog
Rabbit
Turkey
Turtle

Gentleness

Deer
Dolphin
Dove
Fox
Horse
Otter
Porcupine
Rabbit
Skunk
Whale

Grace

Cat
Deer
Dolphin
Dove
Fox
Heron
Mountain Lion
Octopus
Swan
Whale

Gratitude

Buffalo
Deer
Turkey

Grounding or Being Grounded

Cat
Grouse
Heron
Horse
Spider
Turtle

Healing

Badger
Bat
Bear
Dove
Frog
Otter
Raccoon
Raven
Salmon
Snake

Hibernation or Rejuvenation

Badger
Bear
Deer
Frog
Lizard
Salmon
Snake
Squirrel
Swan
Turtle

Home (Strong Ties to or a Pull toward)

Bat
Bee
Dove
Dragonfly
Salmon

Honoring the Sacred

Buffalo
Coyote
Crow
Deer
Eagle
Grouse
Hawk
Raven
Salmon
Spider
Stag
Swan
Turkey
Whale
Wolf

Independence

Badger
Cat
Grouse
Heron
Mountain Lion
Owl

Industriousness, Productivity, or Hard Work

Ant
Beaver
Bee
Mouse
Squirrel

Intelligence

Bear
Coyote
Crow
Dolphin
Dove
Fox
Hawk
Horse
Mountain Lion
Mouse
Octopus
Opossum
Otter
Owl
Raven
Spider
Squirrel
Whale
Wolf

Introspection

Bear
Heron
Owl
Spider

Intuition or Instinct

Cat
Coyote
Crow
Deer
Dog
Hawk
Heron
Lizard
Mountain Lion
Opossum
Owl
Rabbit
Raven
Salmon
Seal
Spider
Squirrel
Whale
Wolf

Job or Career Satisfaction

Ant Beaver
Bee Dog
Horse Otter
Squirrel

Joy

Bee Butterfly
Coyote Crow
Dog Dolphin
Dragonfly Hummingbird
Otter Rabbit
Seal Whale

Leadership

Badger Eagle
Hawk Mountain Lion
Owl Stag

Lightheartedness or Lightness of Being

Butterfly Dragonfly
Hummingbird Otter

Loyalty

Dog Horse

Monogamy

Beaver Coyote
Dove Eagle
Fox Hawk
Otter Raven
Swan Wolf
Wren (Carolina)

Mystery or Magic

Bat
Cat
Crow
Dragonfly
Eagle
Fox
Hummingbird
Mountain Lion
Owl
Raven
Salmon
Snake
Spider
Wren

Nocturnal Habits

Armadillo
Bat
Beaver
Fox
Frog
Mountain Lion
Mouse
Opossum
Owl
Porcupine
Raccoon
Skunk

Obstacles (Overcoming)

Armadillo
Crow
Hawk
Horse
Otter
Salmon
Squirrel

Parental Instincts

Bear
Deer
Moose
Otter
Swan
Turkey
Whale
Wolf

Patience

Cat
Heron
Mountain Lion
Owl
Spider
Turtle

Peacefulness or Tranquility

Butterfly Deer
Dolphin Dove
Heron Swan

Perspective

Bat Dragonfly
Eagle Hawk
Lizard Owl
Raccoon Spider

Planning for the Future

Ant Squirrel

Playfulness

Armadillo Butterfly
Coyote Crow
Dolphin Hummingbird
Otter Porcupine
Raccoon Raven
Seal Skunk
Squirrel Whale
Wolf

Polyamory

Bee Butterfly
Dragonfly Rabbit
Wren

Problem-Solving

Bee Crow
Mouse Octopus
Otter Raccoon
Raven Spider
Squirrel

Protection

Armadillo	Bear
Beaver	Buffalo
Coyote	Dog
Dolphin	Eagle
Moose	Otter
Seal	Stag
Swan	Turtle
Wolf	

Psychic Opening

Bat	Butterfly
Cat	Dolphin
Lizard	Moose
Otter	Owl

Resourcefulness

Crow	Fox
Heron	Mouse
Octopus	Otter
Raccoon	Raven
Squirrel	Wren

Respect

Buffalo	Mountain Lion
Owl	Porcupine
Skunk	Snake
Stag	Wolf

Self-Confidence or Self-Awareness

Badger	Bear
Cat	Crow
Dog	Eagle
Hawk	Heron
Horse	Mountain Lion
Owl	Raven
Salmon	Seal
Skunk	Stag
Swan	Whale
Wolf	

Sense of Humor

Beaver	Coyote
Dolphin	Raven

Sensuality

Cat	Mountain Lion
Otter	Rabbit
Seal	Swan

Shamanic Death or Rebirth

Bat	Bee
Butterfly	Frog
Grouse	Lizard
Opossum	Owl
Salmon	Seal
Snake	Spider
Stag	Swan

Shyness

Armadillo
Bear
Coyote
Deer
Grouse
Mouse
Opossum
Rabbit
Skunk

Solitude or Introversion

Armadillo
Bear
Heron
Moose
Mountain Lion
Mouse
Opossum
Owl
Porcupine
Raccoon
Skunk
Turtle

Standing Up to Adversity

Badger
Bear
Deer
Eagle
Raccoon
Skunk
Squirrel
Stag

Teamwork

Ant
Beaver
Bee
Crow
Dolphin
Horse
Raven
Whale
Wolf

Territorial

Badger
Buffalo
Cat
Dog
Dolphin
Eagle
Hummingbird
Mountain Lion
Mouse
Owl
Rabbit
Seal
Stag
Swan
Wolf
Wren

Time (Perceptions of)

Dragonfly
Frog
Hummingbird
Opossum
Owl
Turtle
Whale

Trance

Bat
Bear
Cat
Heron
Opossum
Owl
Spider
Turtle
Whale

Transformation

Bear
Butterfly
Crow
Dragonfly
Frog
Lizard
Octopus
Rabbit
Salmon
Snake
Swan

Unconditional Love

Deer	Dog
Horse	Otter
Whale	Wolf

ACKNOWLEDGMENTS

To Angela and all the folks at Llewellyn, thank you for making *Chakra Animals* happen!

To the crazy group of alphas who are the brothers and sisters of my Dúshraith family: Kirby (of blessed memory), Tracy, Andrea, Aerianna and Mike, Chelidon and Claudia, Brother Leon, and Roth. We managed to create something indescribable to anyone who wasn't there, and I wouldn't be the person I am today without the love and support of all of you. You are my foundation.

To my earthly family: Corin, Jen, and Turtle. I am so glad you are in my life and that I am part of yours.

To my road tripping, kayaking, wine event, shopping, gab fest, and lots of other fun stuff buddy, Val. Being thrown in an office together all those years ago was the start of a really fabulous friendship! Thanks for being a sister of choice and for being my sounding board on more ideas than I can remember.

To all the animal companions past and present that I have had the honor to share my life with. I may have rescued each of you, but you saved my life in more ways than I can count.

To those who walk with me always: ancestors, spirit guides, angelic ones, and the animals themselves. For whispering in my ear when I'm looking for an answer (usually around 3 a.m.), I thank you.

To the folks at A Feast of Lights 2015 who gave me valuable feedback and suffered through my trial readings, and to Debee, Bernie (of blessed memory), and Michael for buying prototype versions. From the bottom of my heart, I thank you for your belief in this project.

To the organizers of Festival of Light 2015 in Berkeley Springs who welcomed me as a last-minute vendor and to the participants who let me read for you. It was at this event that I received the clarity that I needed to expand the original book. To all the folks who came to my first talk at the 2016 event. I was amazed that Chakra Animals filled the room and that you were so welcoming and engaged. This event will always feel like home to me.

To Sandy of Vermont, thank you for lighting the spark in my brain that eventually became Chakra Animals.

To Geoff and Alice (and, of course, little Maddee) of Portals in Berkeley Springs, thank you for your support and for carrying my stuff.

To Sterling of Crystal Fox in Laurel, thank you for being my initial connection to Llewellyn.

To Thea of New Hampshire, for the phrase "she den."

To Irene of Frederick CUUPS, for suggesting I create decks of cards instead of tokens.

Thank you to several teachers in my past: Ed, for seeing an artist in everyone; Lillian, who taught me to paint with sound; Lorrie and Lenora, for opening my eyes and giving me a love and respect of other cultures (I still have the ram duck planter, Lorrie); and Sherman, in whose class I got my worst grade. The class *A History of Ideas* should be required for anyone breathing. It permanently changed the way I think.

To Ricki and Kathy from my previous day-job life, thank you for being there during the most trying years of my life. I'm so grateful we're still friends.

Thank you to everyone at A-Zone for your understanding during my final edits phase.

And, of course, to my mom.

Finally, to you, the person reading *Chakra Animals*. Thank you for your support!

HOW TO ORDER A DECK OF CARDS

If you would like to order a deck of cards that contains the author's artwork (separate from the art that appears in this book), please visit her Etsy site at www.etsy.com/shop/ChakraAnimals. For updates and announcements, please visit her Chakra Animals Facebook page at https://www.facebook.com/chakraanimals/.

You can also order directly from the manufacturer, or if you are a retailer and want to order several sets, please visit www.makeplayingcards.com/sell/marketplace/chakra-animals-oracle-cards.html.

Please be aware that, in order to save on cost and reduce waste, the cards do not come in a box but are simply shrink-wrapped.

ANIMAL IMAGES

Bee
Buffalo
Butterfly
Cat
Coyote
Crow

Deer
Dog
Dolphin
Dove
Dragonfly
Eagle

Fox
Frog
Grouse
Hawk
Heron
Horse

Hummingbird
Lizard
Moose
Mountain Lion
Mouse
Octopus

Opossum
Otter
Owl
Porcupine
Rabbit
Raccoon

Raven
Salmon
Seal
Skunk
Snake
Spider

Squirrel
Stag
Swan
Turkey

Turtle
Whale
Wolf
Wren

To Write to the Author

If you wish to contact the author or would like more information about this book, please write to the author in care of Llewellyn Worldwide Ltd. and we will forward your request. Both the author and the publisher appreciate hearing from you and learning of your enjoyment of this book and how it has helped you. Llewellyn Worldwide Ltd. cannot guarantee that every letter written to the author can be answered, but all will be forwarded. Please write to:

Angelica Stuart
℅ Llewellyn Worldwide
2143 Wooddale Drive
Woodbury, MN 55125-2989

Please enclose a self-addressed stamped envelope for reply, or $1.00 to cover costs. If outside the U.S.A., enclose an international postal reply coupon.

Many of Llewellyn's authors have websites with additional information and resources. For more information, please visit our website at http://www.llewellyn.com.

Identify, Attune, and Connect to the
Energy of Animals

Animal Frequency

Melissa Alvarez

A REFERENCE TO 200 WILD, DOMESTIC, AND MYTHICAL CREATURES

Animal Frequency

Identify, Attune, and Connect to the Energy of Animals

Melissa Alvarez

Discover the energetic power of animals and how to connect with their frequencies in order to grow spiritually. This easy-to-use, A to Z reference guide contains encyclopedic listings for nearly two hundred animals—wild, domestic, and mythical—and easy techniques and visualizations for building relationships with them, including energetically bonding with your pets. All animals possess a distinctive energy vibration that can connect with yours, allowing you to communicate with them and understand their role in your spiritual development.

978-0-7387-4928-0, 7 ½ x 9 ¼ **$24.99**

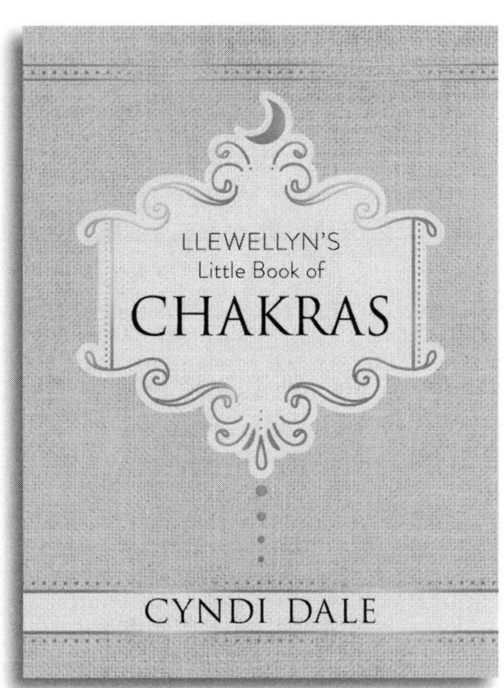
LLEWELLYN'S
Little Book of
CHAKRAS
CYNDI DALE

Llewellyn's Little Book of Chakras
CYNDI DALE

Chakras are subtle energy centers that affect all levels of your being: physical, psychological, and spiritual. In this pocket-size hardcover guide, discover why these spinning wheels of energy are the key to living at your highest potential, with tips for using chakras to:

- Heal from physical and psychological wounds
- Express feelings easily and productively
- Transform work into a joyful vocation
- Solve financial and career difficulties
- Free repressed emotions
- Deal with life's puzzles and predicaments
- Soothe the heart and create more loving relationships

978-0-7387-5155-9, 240 pp., 4 ⅝ x 6 ¼ $12.99

To order, call 1-877-NEW-WRLD or visit llewellyn.com

Prices subject to change without notice

Animal Totem
TAROT
Leeza Robertson
Illustrated by
Eugene Smith

Animal Totem Tarot

LEEZA ROBERTSON

ILLUSTRATED BY EUGENE SMITH

Animal totems are powerful allies and guides for those who seek connection to their abundant energy. Soaring above or swimming below, crawling along the earth or silently stalking in the shadows—all the animals have their own spiritual lessons and insights to help you along your way. In all their grace and wild beauty, animals possess wisdom beyond words. Let them speak to the deepest part of you.

978-0-7387-4348-6, 384-page book and 78-card deck $29.99

New Paths to Animal Totems
Three Alternative Approaches
to Creating Your Own Totemism
Lupa

New Paths to Animal Totems

Three Alternative Approaches to Creating Your Own Totemism

LUPA

Explore three new personalized approaches to animal totemism unlike the usual totem dictionary full of stereotypical meanings. This comprehensive guide gives you a fresh perspective on the foundations, theories, and practices of totemism.

New Paths to Animal Totems presents three unique models of totem work, letting you experiment and blend them into your own spiritual practice. The Correspondence Model enables you to use directions, elements, and more to create your own totemic cosmology. In the Bioregional Model, you'll focus on the local physical and spiritual ecosystems of where you live. Totemism in the Archetypal Model represents aspects of your personality, psyche, and experience.

Each model provides new techniques for exploring totem work, whether you're a beginner or want to invigorate your existing practice. You'll also develop strong relationships and engage in meaningful conversations with your personal animal spirits. Use this essential guidebook to bring strength, wisdom, healing, and positive change to your life with hands-on rituals, meditations, and much more.

978-0-7387-3337-1, 312 pp., 5 3/16 x 8 $16.99